CROSS-CULTURAL PERSPECTIVES ON HUMAN SEXUALITY

Sandra L. Caron
University of Maine

Allyn and Bacon
Boston   London   Toronto   Sydney   Tokyo   Singapore

Copyright © 1998 by Allyn & Bacon
A Viacom Company
160 Gould Street
Needham Heights, MA 02194

Internet: www.abacon.com
America Online: keyword: College Online

A previous edition was published under the same title, copyright © 1997 by Simon & Schuster
Custom Publishing.

ISBN 0-205-27416-1

Printed in the United States of America

10 9 8 7 6 5 4 3 2 1   01 00 99 98 97

THE TABLE OF CONTENTS

PREFACE

Most people could not say that a day goes by in which they do not encounter some aspect of sexuality. We are confronted with issues pertaining to birth control, abortion, AIDS, gay/lesbian rights, and so on in our homes, schools, places of employment and even within our own thoughts. Human sexuality is a widely-discussed topic that often becomes the center of conversation in one form or another. Yet, this topic of discussion should not be limited to one's familiar habitat.

Technological advances in communication and the manner in which we access information has linked us to cultures across the world in ways our ancestors never fathomed. The booming popularity of the Internet, for example, allows us the opportunity to connect with people and places of foreign domain via our own personal computers. College students are quite familiar with this convenient method of communicating since most institutions provide access to the Internet through computer clusters often located in campus libraries. These advances have undoubtedly transformed our world into a global village. Therefore, it has become necessary to learn more about other cultures' social, political, economic, and religious values - and yes, sexual attitudes as well.

The purpose of this book is to serve as a quick reference to facts about cross-cultural perspectives in human sexuality. It can also serve as a supplement to courses taught in human sexuality and cross-cultural psychology or development. It is important to educate Americans of the diverse attitudes and behaviors that exist across the world because knowledge about another culture's views assists us in gaining perspective on our own sexuality.

In addition, this book will help to lessen the ethnocentrism used by many Americans when judging other cultures. In other words, it will assist people in understanding that what goes on in America is not the norm and that our own values should not be treated as the standard by which to judge others. It is natural for Americans to think in such a manner since our country is geographically isolated from nearly 200 nations that exist around the world. Yet, we should not forget that we are indeed a Multicultural nation and a melting pot of different beliefs and practices as well as sexual attitudes. For college students, this fact is apparent since 1 out of every 10 students in American colleges come from other countries. After reading this book, students will learn that sexual behaviors differ among various cultural groups and that there is no set standard for what is considered normal.

This book covers the basic aspects of sexuality for 44 different countries. A brief overview of each country is provided, including information on population, ethnicity, religions, annual income per person (this is the GNP divided by the total population, not average income), etc. It is important to have some background knowledge since the environment we live in often plays a major role in shaping our attitudes on sexuality. Pertinent data is then presented on the following issues: sexual activity, contraception, abortion, sex education, sexually transmitted diseases, homosexuality, prostitution, and pornography. In addition, numerical figures for pregnancies, births, and abortions have been complied and presented at the beginning of the book. Since each chapter follows the same content outline, the reader can easily draw comparisons between each country.

For instance, among industrialized nations, the United States has one of the leading pregnancy rates for teenagers ages 15-19. For every 1,000 American teenage girls, 117 become pregnant each year. Experts who have become long-time advocates of sex education argue that teaching teenagers about human sexuality could help to diminish the pregnancy rate. However, in America, only 23 states require formal teaching about human sexuality. And in many states, these mandates or polices preclude teaching about such subjects as intercourse, abortion, masturbation, homosexuality, condoms, and safer sex.

In comparison, the Netherlands' teenage pregnancy rate stands at 14 per 1,000 teenagers. Ironically, lessons in human sexuality are available at all levels of school education and offered through youth clubs.

Another striking difference relates to abortions. As American politicians continue the controversial debate on the issue, Russians view abortion as a primary method of birth control. On average, every woman born in Russia has four or five abortions. Russia was also the first country in the world to legalize abortion. In Ireland, abortion is illegal except in cases where the mother's life is in danger. In February 1992, a 14-year-old rape victim was prevented by the High Court to travel to Britain for an abortion procedure. This eventually led to a Supreme Court ruling that grants women the freedom to travel abroad and obtain abortions. Presently, an estimated 4,500 Irish women journey to other countries for abortions each year.

While detecting the remarkable differences in sexual behaviors among these 44 countries, the reader will also discover some fascinating similarities. For example, most countries have established a minimum age of sexual consent. Adult pornography is regulated by the government and certain laws control access to sexual material. And in all countries, incest is considered a taboo.

Among the following pages, we present an opportunity to explore various perspectives in human sexuality. The facts presented in this book speak for themselves: We live in a world composed of cultural diversity. It is when we perceive the views of others, we also develop a better understanding of the values and behaviors that exist within our own culture and learn to accept our role in the global village.

About the Authors

When Dr. Sandra L. Caron began seeking materials to instruct a course on cross-cultural perspectives in human sexuality, it was her intent to find an affordable book that addressed such a broad topic. However, she was limited to a collection of articles and books which focused solely on issues such as abortion, pregnancy, and prostitution.

With the assistance of 12 students, Dr. Caron compiled facts and figures and created Cross-Cultural Perspectives in Human Sexuality. This collaborative task began by literally drawing names of countries from a hat. Each student researched at least three countries and presented their findings to their fellow classmates.

Dr. Caron is an Associate Professor of Family Relations and Human Sexuality at the University of Maine. She has served on the Board of Directors for the American Association of Sex Educators, Counselors, and Therapists. While on a six-month sabbatical in Europe, Dr. Caron visited various family planning agencies and exchanged views with sexuality educators from countries such as England, Sweden, Denmark and The Netherlands. In addition, she has worked at Cornell University and

Syracuse University and has conducted hundreds of seminars and workshops on sexuality.

Assisting Dr. Caron in gathering information for this reference book included the following students: Stephanie Bean, Sheryl Brockett, Amanda Corey, Amy Deshane, Allen Ledbetter, Donald McCoy, Jenny Nichols, Andre Pam, Lynn Reed, Rachel Riley, Roberta Smith, and Anthony Wright. Nancy M. Lewis, Social Science and Humanities Reference Librarian at the University of Maine, provided pregnancy, birth, and abortion data for each of the 44 countries mentioned in this book.

PREGNANCY, BIRTH AND ABORTION DATA
By country, per 1000 women
Compiled by Nancy M. Lewis
January 1997, rev. March 1997

Country	Abortions	Births	Pregnancies
Australia			
15-19	-------	20.5(a)1993	-------
15-44	16.6(b)1994	63.3(a)1993	29.2(c)1993
Austria			
15-19	-------	23.0(d)1992	-------
15-44	-------	54.9(d)1992	23.4(e)1992
Belgium			
15-19	-------	12(f)1994	-------
15-44	5.1(g)1985	22.4(h)1995	24.4(e)1990
Brazil			
15-19	-------	51.2(d)1990	-------
15-44	-------	66.4(d)1990	32.4(e)1990
Bulgaria			
15-19	21.3(a)1992	33.6(a)1992	-------
15-44	37.8(a)1992	24.8(a)1992	20.7(c)1992
Canada			
15-19	15.4(j)1991	27(k)1990-95	-------
15-44	14.7(j)1991	-------	-------
Chile			
15-19	-------	63.5(m)1991	-------
15-44	32.2(n)1987	87.4(m)1991	42.3(p)1991
China			
15-19	-------	11.7(q)1994	-------
15-44	37.5(b)1994	1136.7(q)1994	-------
Costa Rica			
15-19	-------	85(f)1994	-------
15-44	-------	50.4(h)1995	-------
Cuba			
15-19	-------	64.5(r)1991	-------
15-44	56.5(b)1994	62.4(r)1991	35.7(s)1990
Czech Republic			
15-19	24.2(a)1991	42.8(a)1991	-------
15-44	46.8(a)1991	53.7(a)1991	22.9(c)1991
Denmark			
15-19	15.7(a)1992	9.8(a)1992	-------
15-44	16.8(a)1992	60.8(a)1992	26.0(c)1992

Egypt			
15-19	-------	75(f)1994	-------
15-44	-------	60.4(h)1995	61.6(t)1991
Finland			
15-19	13.4(m)1990	12.3(m)1990	-------
15-44	10.9(m)1990	59.4(m)1990	25.6(p)1990
France			
15-19	-------	9.1(m)1991	43(u)1990
15-44	13.2(g)1988	60.1(m)1991	26.3(p)1991
Germany			
15-19	-------	16(f)1994	-------
15-44	8.7(b)1994	21.4(h)1995	-------
Greece			
15-19	-------	15.0(a)1993	-------
15-44	2.3(v)1990	46.0(a)1993	46.4(c)1993
Hungary			
15-19	30.5(a)1993	34.0(a)1993	-------
15-44	33.4(a)1993	52.3(a)1993	21.9(c)1993
India			
15-19	1.0(w)1990	73(f)1994	-------
15-44	2.7(w)1990	57.4(h)1995	-------
Iran			
15-19	-------	115(f)1994	-------
15-44	-------	71.4(h)1995	-------
Ireland			
15-19	-------	10.2(x)1991	-------
15-44	5.4(y)1994	32.5(x)1991	29.9(z)1991
Israel			
15-19	8.1(d)1992	19.6(d)1992	-------
15-44	14.8(d)1992	96.1(d)1992	42.7(z)1991
Italy			
15-19	5.5(d)1991	10(f)1994	-------
15-44	10.1(aa)1993	21.1(h)1995	19.0(e)1991
Japan			
15-19	-------	3.9(a)1993	-------
15-44	14.5(b)1994	44.9(a)1993	19.4(bb)1993
Kenya			
15-19	-------	132(f)1994	-------
15-44	25(cc)1990	82.9(h)1995	-------

Mexico			
15-19	-------	71(f)1994	-------
15-44	-------	52.6(h)1995	66.6(e)1990
Netherlands			
15-19	14(dd)1990	6.4(u)1990	14(u)1990
15-44	5.2(g)1990	24.6(h)1995	25.5(c)1993
New Zealand			
15-19	16.2(ee)1992	15.7(d)1992	-------
15-44	14.0(ff)1992	35.6(d)1992	34.1(gg)1992
Norway			
15-19	18.7(d)1992	7.3(d)1992	-------
15-44	16.3(d)1992	31.2(d)1992	27.9(e)1992
Poland			
15-19	-------	31.6(d)1991	-------
15-44	3.6(b)1994	63.5(d)1991	-------
Portugal			
15-19	-------	22.5(a)1993	-------
15-44	-------	51.2(a)1993	22.4(c)1993
Romania			
15-19	41.8(a)1993	47.0(a)1993	-------
15-44	116.0(a)1993	49.6(a)1993	21.7(c)1993
Russia			
15-19	-------	46.3(a)1993	-------
15-44	119.6(b)1994	41.4(a)1993	17.7(c)1993
Singapore			
15-19	14.9(a)1994	7.5(a)1994	-------
15-44	20.4(a)1994	64.8(a)1994	35.4(v)1993
Slovakia			
15-19	14.4(a)1991	50.4(r)1991	-------
15-44	38.4(a)1991	70.0(r)1991	29.2(v)1991
South Africa			
15-19	-------	330(hh)1995	-------
15-44	-------	66.1(h)1995	-------
Spain			
15-19	-------	15(f)1994	-------
15-44	4.8(g)1991	22(h)1995	20.3(s)1990
Sweden			
15-19	18.4(a)1993	11.2(a)1993	-------
15-44	19.5(a)1993	68.4(a)1993	26.8(c)1993

Switzerland			
15-19	-------	6.8(a)1993	-------
15-44	8.7(g)1990	55.2(a)1993	23.7(c)1993
Thailand			
15-19	-------	40.4(r)1992	-------
15-44	-------	64.0(r)1992	33.5(v)1992
Turkey			
15-19	-------	57(f)1994	-------
15-44	2.8(g)1991	25.3(h)1995	-------
United Kingdom			
15-19	18.7(r)1992	30.7(a)1993	-------
15-44	13.8(r)1992	62.3(a)1993	-------
United States			
15-19	55.0(kk)1991	60.7(jj)1992	117.0(mm)1990
15-44	25.9(jj)1992	68.9(jj)1992	109.9(jj)1992
Zimbabwe			
15-19	-------	96(f)1994	-------
15-44	-------	36.4(h)1995	-------

a)   United Nations. Department for Economic & Social Information & Policy Analysis. Demographic Yearbook. 1994.

b)   Dorgan, Charity Anne, ed. Statistical Record of Health & Medicine. Gale Research Inc., 1995.

c)   United Nations. 1994. Data for women of all ages.

d)   ------. 1993.

e)   ------. 1993. Data for women of all ages.

f)   United States. Bureau of the Census. World Demographic Data, Feburary 1994.

g)   Abortion Policies: a Global Review. United Nations, Department of Economic & Social Development, 1992.

h)   United States. Central Intelligence Agency. The World Factbook 1995. Http:/www.odci.gov/cia/publications/95fact/.   Published July 1995.

j)   Wadhera, Surinder. Selected Therapeutic Abortion Statistics, 1970-1991. Statistics Canada, 1994.

k)   The Progress of Nations. United Nations, Population Divisions. Http://www.unicef.org/pon96/inbirth.htm. Viewed December 27, 1996.

m)   United Nations. 1991 & 1993.

n)   A Matter of Fact, v. 19. Pierian Press. 1993. Data per 1000 women of reproductive age.

p)   United Nations. 1991 & 1993. Data for women of all ages.

q)   People's Republic of China. State Statistical Bureau. China Statistical Yearbook. 1995.

r)   United Nations. 1993 & 1994.

s)   -----. 1992 & 1993. Data for women of all ages.

t)   -----. 1991 & 1994. Data for women of all ages.

u)   Narring, Francoise, Pierre-Andre Michaud, and Vinit Sharma. "Demographic and Behavioral Factors Associated with Adolescent Pregnancy in Switzerland." Family Planning Perspectives. 28(5):232-36. September/October 1992.

v)   United Nations. 1993 & 1994. Data for women of all ages.

w)   -----. 1990 & 1993.

x)   -----. 1992 & 1993.

y)   Dorgan, 1995. Data based on abortions obtained in England & Wales.

z)   United Nations. 1992 & 1993. Data for women of all ages.

a a)   National Institute of Statistics of Italy. Statistical Data About Italy. Http://sunsite.sut.ac.jp/embitaly/ItalFiles/Statis_Sata.html/#8.   Viewed December 24, 1996. Data per 100 women ages 15-49.

b b)   Japan. Statistics Bureau. Management & Coordination Agency. Japan Statistical Yearbook. 1996. For women of all ages.

c c)   "Proximate Determinants of Fertility", p. 103. In Population Dynamics of Kenya, ed. by William Brass & Carole L. Jolly, National Academy Press, 1993. Data for women of all ages.

dd)   A Matter of Fact, v. 12-13. 1990. Data per 1000 adolescents

e e)   United Nations. 1993. Data for women 16-19.

f f)   -----. 1993. Data for women 16-44.

g g)   Statistics New Zealand. New Zealand Official Yearbook. 1995. Data for women of all ages.

h h)   South African Ministry for Welfare & Population Development. Population Policy for South Africa? Http://www.polity.org.za/govdocs/green_papers/population.html. Published April 20, 1995.

jj)   Statistical Abstract of the United States. Government Printing Office, 1996.

k k)   Morbidity and Mortality Weekly Report. v.42. U.S. Department of Health, Education and Welfare, Public Health Service, Center for Disease Control, 1993.

m m)   Sex and America's Teenagers. New York: Alan Guttmacher Institute, 1994. Data extrapolated using 1982-1988 trend.

AUSTRALIA
POPULATION: 17,086,000

Capital:
Canberra
(population: 289,000)

Major Cities & Population: Sydney 3.5 million; Melbourne 2.9 million; Brisbane 1.2 million; Perth 1 million; Adelaide 1 million

Ethnic Groups: White 95%; Asian 4%; Aboriginal 1%

Languages: English (official) and aboriginal language

Major Religions: Anglican 26%, Roman Catholic 26%, other Christian 24%

Annual Income Per Person: $16,590

Urban Population: 86%

Infant Mortality: 7 per 1,000 births

Life Expectancy: Females 80 yrs, Males 74 yrs

Adult Literacy: 99%

Health Care: 1 physician per 438 people. Universal health insurance has been available since 1984; private health insurance is also available.

References:
The Europa World Year Book (1995). Europa Publications Limited.
Encyclopedic World Atlas (1994). NY: Oxford University Press.

Sexual Activity

* The average age of first sexual intercourse in Australia is 16.6 years old.[1]

Contraception

* The most commonly used methods of contraception are the pill, IUD, condom, and diaphragm.[2]
* A major problem in Australia is premature discontinuation of contraceptives, usually due to side effects and dissatisfaction.[2]
* Lack of education and religion also influence the utilization of contraceptives in Australia.[2]
* Indirect support is provided by the government toward contraceptive use.[3]

Abortion[3]

* Only South Australian and Northern Territory laws define lawful abortions. Other states and territories derive laws from judicial interpretation.
* All states permit abortions to save the life of the pregnant woman.
* All states and territories require that abortions be performed in a hospital and by licensed physicians.
* The Australian government health insurance benefits available to all citizens, cover legal abortions.
* All states except for Tasmania (Criminal Code Act of 1924) and Western Australia (Criminal Code Act of 1913) permit abortions on mental and physical health grounds.
* The maximum prison term for persons performing illegal abortions range from 10-15 years.

Sex Education[4]

* Health Minister Brian Howe released a report recommending installing a condom vending machine in schools as part of sex education.
* Many state education officials agreed to read the report and considered integrating condom use and sexuality into their AIDS education material.
* Schools run by the Roman Catholic Church agreed to focus on improving AIDS education but not sex education or condom use.

STDs, including AIDS

* From 1982 to the end of March 1992, 3,160 cases of AIDS were diagnosed.[5]
* 97% of cases were in men, of whom 91% were adults or adolescents reporting homosexual contact.[5]
* In women 40% of cases were acquired through receipt of blood.[5]
* Transmission of HIV among people with AIDS in Australia has been attributed to sexual contact between men.[5]
* The number of cases of Syphilis: 2,293, Hepatitis B: 2,254, Gonorrhea: 2,805 and Chlamydia: 6,493.[6]

Homosexuality

* In 1970 homosexuals established an open organization to demand recognition, equal and just treatment before the law, and an end to discrimination.[7]
* In 1972 South Australia became the first state to partially decriminalize homosexual acts.[7]
* By 1987 all the states of Australia decriminalized homosexual acts except for Queensland which has made no attempt.[7]
* On Nov. 23, 1992 the Australian cabinet ended its ban on homosexuals in the military.[8]
* Based on a study performed by M. Ross he estimated that one in 24 married men will have sexual contact with another man.[9]

Prostitution[10]

* Prostitution itself is legal in Australia, but street prostitution is illegal in New South Wales and Queensland.
* Prostitution is not illegal in these areas for the client.
* There are laws against pimping and procuring.
* The age of consent is 16 years old for women who can be with a prostitute.
* Prostitutes must be 18 years old or older.
* The average hourly rate for prostitutes is $150-$200.
* New South Wales does allow licensed brothels. These brothels or massage parlors require health checks from their employees. But these women cannot reject clients and they are required to sign a contract waiving their civil rights and entitlement to health & safety protection.
* Condoms are compulsory in sexual relationships with prostitutes.

Pornography

* Child pornography in Australia is a federal offense and is punishable under Australian law.[11]
* Australia classifies all films and literature to protect children from pornographic material.[12]
* The classifications range from G (general exhibition) to X (explicit sex: restricted to adults 18 and over).[12]
* The government cannot impose restrictions on what can be filmed, but can restrict transportation of obscene material.[12]
* X rated videos are not illegal in Australia but to sell them commercially is illegal.[12]

Resources

Australian Association of Sex Educators, Counselors, and Therapists (AASERT), P.O. Box 346, Lane Cove NSW. 2066.

Family Planning Australia, Inc., Lua Building, Suite 3, First Floor, 39 Geils L, P.O. Box 9026, Deakin, ACT

References

1. C.M. Tomlinson, "Studying Australia - Beyond the Textbook Approach", The Social Studies, Vol. 79 (1988) pp. 32-37.

2. M. Bracher, "Premature Discontinuation of Contraception in Australia", Family Planning Perspectives, March/April (1992).

3. United Nations, Vol. 1, Abortion Policies: A Global Review, (New York, 1992).

4. "Condom Sales in Schools Considered", Facts on File, V52, n268S, p. 336, May (1992).

5. J. Kaldor, "The Acquired Immunodeficiency Syndrome in Australia: Incidence 1982-1991," Journal of the American Medical Association, March (1993).

6. Yearbook of Australia, (Canberra: Commonwealth of Australia, 1996), Table 8.11.

7. D. Wayne (editor), Encyclopedia of Homosexuality, (NY: Guilford, 1990).

8. "Australia Ends a Prohibition on Homosexuals in Military", New York Times, Nov. 24 (1992).

9. R. Tielman, M. Carballo, & A. Hendriks (editors), Bisexuality and HIV/AIDS, (NY:Promotheus Books, 1991) pp. 127-129.

10. The World Sex Guide. Last updated: 1996/04/30. (C) 1994-96 Atta and M. <an48932@anon.penet.fi>. (retrieved June 26, 1996)

11. Liberal and National Parties Law and Justice Policy, (Feb. 1996), http://www.liberal.org.au/policy/law/lawjstce.htm. (retrieved June 26, 1996)

12. FAQ v5.65 11/12: Legal Issues, (retrieved June 26, 1996) http://www.ext/faq/usenet/alt.sex/movies/part11/faq.html.

AUSTRIA
POPULATION: 7.7 MILLION

Capital:
Vienna
(population: 1,483,000)

Major Cities & Populations   Vienna 1.4 million; Graz 243,00; Linz 200,000; Sulzburg 139,000; Innsbruck 117,000

Ethnic Groups: Austrian 96%; Yugoslavian 2%; Turkish

Languages: German 94% (offical); Solvene; Croat; Turkish; Slovak; Magyar

Major Religions: Roman Catholic 84%; Protestant 6%

Annual Income per Person: $20,380

Urban Population: 54%

Infant Mortality: 9 per 1,000 births

Life Expectancy: Female 79 years; Male 72 years

Adult Literacy: 99%

Health Care System: National health care system, with nearly universal access. 1 doctor per 327 persons; 1 bed per 105 persons

References:
Encyclopedic World Atlas (1994) NY: Oxford University Press.
The World Almanac and Book of Facts (1995) Mahwah, NJ: World Almanac Books
"Austria" The CIA Factbook,   http://www.odcl.gov/cia/publications/95fact/ch.html.

Sexual Activity

* Age of consent for heterosexual relations is 14.[1]
* One third of the women have had sexual intercourse before the age of 16 years.[2]
* Twenty-four percent of 15-44 year olds have had at least one unplanned pregnancy, and 10% have had more than one.[2]

Contraception

* In general the standard of contraception in Austria is rather low; on average only every second Austrian woman uses contraceptives. No data is available on the use of prophylactics by Austrian men.[3]
* First Love is an Austrian FPA counselling center dedicated to helping young people. First Love offers free and confidential psychological counselling and gynecolgical examinations to young women, one afternoon per week.[4]
* Contraceptives are not supplied free of charge through the State services. Condoms are advertised and available in pharmacies and condom vending machines also exist. There are no practical obstacles to obtaining contraceptives except for adolescents who may not be welcomed by all physicians.[5]
* Percentage of contraceptive methods used in Austria: 18% None, 7% Rhythm, 5% Withdrawal, 16% Barrier, 7% IUD, 42% Pill, 5% Sterilization.[6]
* Vasectomies as well as vasectomy-reversal procedures are performed less frequently in Austria than in other European countries.[2]

Abortion[7]

* Since January 1974 abortion on request within the first trimester of pregnancy has been exempt from punishment for the first time in Austrian history.
* Although abortion within the first trimester is legal, access to abortion is still not guaranteed throughout Austria. In several parts of the country it is difficult or simply impossible to obtain one because many physicians refuse to perfom abortions for moral and/or religious reasons.
* All abortions must be performed by a licensed physician. The majority of abortions are performed by doctors in private practices.
* The cost of abortion is relatively high. It is typically paid for by the consumer.

Sex Education[8]

* Sex eduacation is legally regulated as part of the school curriculum and it is theoretically implemented in elementary, secondary, and higher education levels.
* The situation is not reflected in practice, though some sex education is available in some schools according to the willingness of the teaching staff. The mass media regularly feature sex education.

STDs, including AIDS[9]

* There have been 1,488 cases of AIDS reported to date.

Homosexuality

* In Austria, promotion or encouraging of homosexuality is forbidden and lesbian and gay organizations are prohibited.[10]
* Lesbian organizations and publications are illegal under Sections 220 and 221 of the Penal Code.[11]
* Austria allows persons who engage in homosexual behavior to serve in the military.[12]
* The age of consent for a homosexual male is 18, but for lesbian females it is 14.[13]
* Artificial insemination is no longer available to lesbians and donation of ova is outlawed.[2]

Prostitution

* Prostitution is legal in all but one province, Vorarlberl.[14]
* In Vienna, legalized prostitution is tightly controlled by the Board of the Viennese Public Health Service. Registered prostitutes are routinely screened for all important STDs, such as syphilis, HIV, gonorrrhea, Chlamydial, yeast infections, and Trichomonas vaginalis. Futhermore, cytological smears are obtained from the cervix and chest X-rays are performed at least once a year.[15]
* Those found to be HIV-positive are prohibited from working.[2]

Pornography

* No information available.

Resources

* Osterreichische Gesellschaft fur Familieplanung, Semmelweis Frauenklinik Bastiengasse 36-38, 1180 Vienna.

References

1. Alan F. Reekie, "Age of Consent Laws in the Council of Europe States in 1993," <http://ftp.tcp.com/qrd/world/europe/age.of.consent.laws-12.20.94>.

2. Bennett, C.L., Schwartz, B., & Marberger, M. (1993). Health care in Austria: Universal access, national health insurance and private health. JAMA, 269 (21), 2798-2804.

3. Rolston & Eggert, "Abortion In The New Europe" A Comparative Handbook,(Westport, CT., 1994).

4. G. Traun-Vogt & W. Kostenwein, "First Love and Heart Beat in Austria," Choices (1996), 25(1), pp. 15.

5. P. Meredith & L. Thomas, "Planned Parenthood In Europe"A Human Rights Perspective, (NH. 1986) p.61.

6. K. Knewman, "The Contraceptive Situation in Europe," Progress Postponed: Abortion in Europe in the 1990's (1993) p. 11.

7. United Nations, Abortion Policies: A Global Review, (NY. 1992) pp.32-33.

8. P. Meredith & L. Thomas, "Planned Parenthood In Europe" A Human Rights Perspective, (NH. 1986) p.63.

9. HIV.NET "Epidemiology: Transmission Cases" http://www.hiv.net (retrieved June 26, 1996)

10. http:www.quality.org/FQRD/assocs/ilgal/euroletter/35-Survey.html/

11. Snyder, P. (19992). The European Women's Almanac. New York, NY: Columbia University Press. p. 26.

12. S. Harris, "Military Polices Regarding Behavior: An International Survey," Journal of Homosexuality, Vol. 21 (4) (1991) p. 67-74.

13. R. Wockner, "European Laws On Gay Sex Vary," International News CA. (June 17, 1996), p. 1.

14. The World Sex Guide. Last update 1996/04/30. (c) 1994,1995,1996 Atta and M. <an48932@anon.penet.fi>

15. A. Stary & W. Kopp, "Sexualy Transmitted Diseases," 18:3, MedGate Access Plan, Jul-Sep(1991) p. 159-65.

9

BELGIUM
POPULATION: 10,081,880

Capital:
Brussels
(population: 950,000)

Major Cities & Populations: Antwerp 465,000;   Ghent 230,000
Charleroi 207,000; Liege 197,000

Ethnic Groups: Fleming 55%;   Walloon 33%

Languages: Flemish (Dutch) 56%;   French 32%;
German

Major Religions: Roman Catholic 75%

Annual Income per Person: $17,700

Urban Population: 97%

Infant Mortality: 7 per 1,000 births

Life Expectancy: Female 81 years;   male 74 years

Adult Literacy: 98%

Health Care System: Physicians: 1 per 278 persons

References:
Encyclopedic World Atlas (1994) NY: Oxford University Press
The World Almanac and Book of Facts 1996 (1995) Mahwah, NJ: World Almanac Books

Sexual Activity[1]

* The age of consent is 16.

Contraception[2]

* Almost every woman obtaining an abortion is given a prescription for contraceptives following the procedure.
* Contraceptive prevalence in Belgium is high. Results from a study of 1,050 women aged 15-44 showed that 68 percent use a contraceptive method, as follows: the pill, 46 percent; IUD, 8 percent; sterilization, 8 percent; condom, 3 percent; withdrawal, 1 percent; periodic abstinence, 1 percent; diaphragm, injectibles, spermicides, <1 percent.

Abortion[2]

* RU-486 (the "abortion pill") is not available in Belgium.
* Until April 1990 abortion was illegal in Belgium under all circumstances. However, a small group of health professionals had long provided high-quality abortion services in outpatient facilities and in hospitals.
* The 1867 Belgian Penal Code, which defined the pre-1990 abortion law, was based on the Napoleonic Code of 1810, and it restricted abortion under all circumstances.
* In April 1990 the Belgian Parliament approved a law that permits abortion within the first 12 weeks of pregnancy when a physician deems the woman to be in a "state of distress"- a condition that is legally undefined.
* After 12 weeks of pregnancy, abortion can be performed if two physicians agree that the woman's health is in danger, or in cases of proved fetal malformation.
* A six-day waiting period is required from the time of the request to the time of the procedure.
* Access to legal abortion remains more difficult for Flemish women than for French-speaking women, because of the more conservative social climate in Flander and the influence of Catholicism there.
* The abortion ratio is approximately 13 per 100 live births.
* The very low admission rates for corresponding gynecological emergencies in public hospitals suggest that "back street abortions" are rare.
* The new Belgian legislation does not explicitly require parental consent for minors under the age of 18, but some abortion service providers try

to obtain such consent, not differentiating abortion from other medical procedures that require consent.
* Most patients pay around US$120 for the complete abortion procedure, after reimbursement from medical insurance.

Sex Education

* In Belgium, health education and prevention now come under the responsibility of the Communities (French-speaking, Flemish and German-speaking), rather than that of the national state.[3]
* Flemish Belgium referred to the introduction of new school programs on AIDS Prevention and Education on Sexuality and Relationships.[4]
* In Belgium, sex education is not particularly linked to a special school subject and it may be an element of any subject, and it happens during a student's pre-adolescence.[4]

STDs, Including AIDS[5]

* Currently, there are 2,152 reported cases of AIDS in Belgium.

Homosexuality

* Legislation: In 1795 the French invaded the Code Penalfo 1791 on Belgian territory: sexual activity between people of the same sex was no longer a crime as long as it was pursued among adults and in private.[6]
* A success of gay activism in Belgium was the repeal in 1986 of the article 372bis of the penal code, which had been introduced in 1965 stipulating eighteen instead of sixteen as the age of consent for homosexual contact.[6]
* There is no discrimination against homosexuals inthe armed forces.[7]

Prostitution[1]

* Prostitution is illegal, but tolerated. Only pimping and trade in women is prosecuted. Until the fifties, there was an official prostitution policy with registration and health checks. That was abolished, but certain cities have reimplemented this policy unofficially.

Pornography

* The legal age for viewing pornography in Belgium is 18 years.[8]
* Sex shops and peep shows have been tolerated for the past 3-5 years in larger citites.[1]
* XXX videos are shown in some brothels.[1]

Resources

Belgium (Flemish), Federatie Centra Voor, Geboortenregeling en Sexsuele, Opvoeding, Meersstraat 138 B, 9000 Gent, Tel: (32 9) 221 0722, Fax: (32 9) 220 8406.

Belgium (French), Fédération Belge pour le Planning Familial et l'Education Sexuelle, 34 rue de la Tulipe, 1050 Brussels, Tel: (32 2) 502 8203, Fax: (32 2) 502 5613.

References

1. The World Sex Guide, "Prostitution in: Belgium," http://www.paranoia.com/faq/ prostitution/Belgium.html, last update: 1996/04/30, (C) 1994, 1995, 1996, Atta and M. <an48932@anon.penet.fi>, received 6/18/96.

2. F. Donnay (1993). Safe Abortions in an Illegal Context: Perceptions from Service Providers in Belgium. Studies in Family Planning, 24 (3), p. 150-157.

3. A. Cherbonnier, (1990). Belgium: A Training Programme in AIDS Prevention. Planned Parenthood in Europe, 19(1), p. 17.

4. D. Vilar, (1994). School Sex Education: Still a Priority in Europe, Planned Parenthood in Europe, 23(3), p. 8.

5. HIV.NET, Wir freuen uns auf Ihren Kommentar zu HIV.NET., Seinhäuser Verlag, Internet-Abteilung, Telefax: 0202/613704, Copyright © 1996, Seinhäuser Verlag, 21.03.96, http://hiv.net/hiv/epidem/table.t3_1.htm, received 6/19/96.

6. W. Dynes (1990). Encyclopedia of Homosexuality, NY: Garland Pub, p. 124-125.

7. Alan F. Reekie, "Age of Consent Laws in the Council of Europe States in 1993," <http://ftp.tcp.com/qrd/world/europe/age.of.consent.laws-12.20.94>.

8. Pornography, "Restricted Access," http://www.pinkboard.com.au:80/r.html, received 6/19/96.

BRAZIL
POPULATION: 153,322,000

Capital:
Brasilia
(population 1,577,000)

Major Cities & Population:	Sao Paulo 16.8 million; Rio de Janeiro 11 million; Belo Horizonte 3.4 million; Recife 2.9 million; Porto Alegre 2.9 million; Salvador 2.3 million; Fortaleya 2 million
Ethnic Groups:	White 53%; Mulatto 22%; Mestizo 12%; Black 11%; Indian 1%
Languages:	Portuguese is the official language; Plus Spanish, English and French
Major Religions:	Roman Catholic 87%, Protestant 8%
Annual Income Per Person:	$2,920
Urban Population:	77%
Infant Mortality:	57 per 1,000 live births
Life Expectancy:	Females 69 yrs, males 64 yrs
Adult Literacy:	80%
Health Care:	Publicly funded clinics & health centers. 1 physician per 848 people

---

References:
Encyclopedic World Atlas. (1994). NY: Oxford University Press.
The World Almanac and Book of Facts 1996. (1995). Mahwah, NJ: World Almanac Books.

15

Sexual Activity

* Brazilians are having sexual relations 1.6 times a week. This is half the rate of three times a week which was occurring five years ago.[1]
* Economic hardship along with the rise in HIV have contributed to the reduction in sexual relations.[1]
* Median age of first intercourse is 16 years old.[2]
* 15% of the 14,000 11-14 year olds who become pregnant each year in Brazil have been rape.[3]

Contraception

* In 1979 the advertising of contraceptives was decriminalized and the distribution of contraceptives was permitted.[4]
* The government in Brazil is not involved in a public system for delivery of contraceptives or the funding of contraceptives.[5]
* Sterilization is one of the top forms of birth control in Brazil, but it is illegal. President Fernando Henrique Cardosa is currently urging Congress to make the procedure legal. This bill will authorize hospitals to sterilize men and women over the age of 25 who have more than two children.[6]
* Most popular methods: female sterilization 44.4%, pill 41%, vasectomy 9%, abstinence and withdrawal 6.2%, condoms 2.5%, IUD 1.5%, other 3.5%.[7]
* Within the public sector contraceptives are delivered through the PAISM and PROSAD programs.[8]
* Emergency contraceptives are available in Brazil in the form of a pill known as Postinor.[8]

Abortion

* The performance of an abortion constitutes a criminal act in Brazil, but is permitted to save the life of the women and to terminate a pregnancy resulting from rape.[9]
* In Brazil 88% of the population is Catholic, giving them influence over health care as well as abortion.[10]
* It is estimated that 4 million abortions are performed annually.[3]
* Under the Penal Code if a pregnant woman performs an abortion upon herself or consents to its performance she is subject to a sentence of one to three years of detention.[11]
* An abortion performed upon a woman without her consent is punishable up to 10 years in prison.[12]

* Many women are taking Misoprastol to induce an abortion. This is an ulcer drug that until 1991 was sold without a prescription.[13]

Sex Education[14]

* In 1993 a poll implemented by the mainstream newspaper in Brazil showed that 86% of the respondents wanted sex education in schools.
* Non governmental organizations (NGO's) have recently begun developing sex education programs in public and private schools.
* One organization known as GTPOS has in the past 8 years implemented sexual guidance programs.
* GTPOS believes that sexual guidance programs should begin in preschool and continue through high school.
* GTPOS has trained teachers in this area and focused on education as well as prevention.

STDs, including AIDS

* Brazil has one of the highest rates of HIV/AIDS prevalence in the world. They rank third in the number of AIDS cases after sub-Saharan Africa and the U.S.[15]
* It is estimated that out of the 158 million people, 1 million are HIV positive.[15]
* 22% of the people who are infected with AIDS are women.[16]
* Under the Penal Code it is illegal to expose someone by means of sexual relations to a venereal disease when the perpetrator is aware of their disease.[4]
* If the person intentionally inflicts a venereal disease they are punishable up to 4 years in prison.[2]

Homosexuality

* Four gay groups in Brazil still remain and are legally recognized.[17]
* Homosexuality is legal in Brazil.[17]
* Brazil does display very ambiguous opinions regarding homosexuality: on one hand it is a nation with an exuberant gay culture.[18]
* One homosexual is murdered in Brazil every 5 days.[18]
* There have been 1,200 killings of homosexuals since 1980.[18]
* Bisexual behavior is quite prevalent in Brazil, a country where men are not considered to be gay if they have sex with women as well as men, or if they take a "dominant" role in sexual acts with other male.[19]

Prostitution

* Prostitution in Brazil is legal but pimping and trading in women is illegal.[20]
* Maintaining a place for sexual liaisons is illegal.[20]
* In Brazil there are street prostitutes, women working out of bars, hotels, massage parlors, saunas, and escort services.[20]
* Child prostitution is an expanding market in Brazil. There are between 250,000 and 500,000 children involved in the sex trade.[21]
* Some children work in brothels and service 10 to 15 clients a day, and some are sold to ranchers who gang rape them to death.[21]

Pornography[22]

* Legal age for viewing pornography in Brazil is 18 years old.
* No law exists in Brazil regarding production of pornographic materials.

Resources

*Associacao Brasieira de Sexologia, Rua Tamandare 693-Conj. 31, Sao Paulo.
*Centro de Sexolgia de Brasilia, SHIS-QI-19, Conjunto 10, Casa 6, Brasilia, DF.
*Grupo Transas do Corpo Acoes Educativas em Saude e Sexualidade (GTC/AESS), Av. Anhanguera, No. 5674 Sala 1304 Centro, 74039-900 Goiania-Go.
*Sociedade Brasileira de Sexualidade Humana, Rua Amancio Moro, 77 Alto da Gloria Curtiba, Parana, 80030.
*Sociedade Brasileira de Sexolgia, Praca Serzedelo Correia 15, Apt. 703, Copacabana, Rio de Janeiro, 22040.

References

1. Brooke, J. (January, 1994). "Economy dampens ardor of Brazilians," New York Times.
2. Population Reports, Series J, No. 41, Oct. (1995).
3. Schmittroth, L. (1995). Statistical Record of Women Worldwide. New York, NY: Gale Research. p. 614, Table 642.
4. J. Masur, <jmkm@echonyc.com>, Center for Reproductive Law & Policy, 1995.
5. Constitucao da Republica Federativa do Brazil (1988), translated in The Constitution of the Federative Republic of Brazil, 1988, in Constitutions of the Countries of the World 112 (Albert P. Blaustein and Gilbert H. Flanz eds., 1993).
6. "Brazilian president agrees to back voluntary sterilization," Contemporary Issues in Sexuality, Vol. 30 No. 3 March (1996).
7. Harris, R. (September 1994). "Despite ban, sterilization big in Brazil," Los Angeles Times, Vol. 113.
8. UNFP, Contraceptive Requirements and Logistics Management Needs in Brazil, Technical Report No. 21, 7 (1995).
9. Boland, R. (1993). The current status of abortion laws in Latin America: Prospects & strategies for change. The Journal of Law, Medicine and Ethics 69.
10. Foy, F.A. (1995), 1995 Catholic Almanac, pg. 332.
11. Penal Code, Special Pt., Title I - Crimes Against the Person, ch. I -Crimes Against Life, at Article 124.
12. Penal Code, Special Pt., Title I - Crimes Against the Person, ch. I -Crimes Against Life, at Article 125.
13. "Ulcer drug used for abortions in Brazil," Contemporary Issues in Sexuality, Vol. 25 No. 7, July (1993).
14. Egypto, A.C, Pinto, M.C. & Bock, S.D. (1996). Brazilian organization develops sexual guidance programs, SIECUS Report, Feb/March.
15. "Sexual culture in Brazil", Contemporary Issues in Sexuality, 29(4), April, 1995.
16. Brazil - Health: AIDS Increasing Among Sterilized Women, Inter Press Service (Rio de Janeiro), May 5, 1994.
17. Yayne, D. (1990), Encyclopedia of Homosexuality, New York: Guilford.
18. Brooke, J (Aug, 1993). In live and let live land, gay people are slain. New York Times.
19. Kelly, G. (1996). Sexuality Today. Guilford, CT: Brown & Benchmark. p. 530.
20. The World Sex Guide. Last updated: 1996/04/30. (C) 1994, 1995, 1996 atta and M. <an48932@anon.penet.fi>.
21. Sachs, A. (July/Aug 1994). Child prostitution in the developing world. World Watch.
22. http://www.pinkboard.com.au:80/r.html, 6-19-96.

BULGARIA
POPULATION: 9 MILLION

Capital:
Sofia
(Population 289,000)

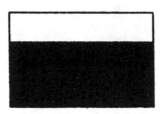

Major Cities & Population:	Sofia 1.1 million, Ploudiv 357,000, Vaina 306,000, Burgas 198,000
Languages:	Bulgarian Turkish, Romany
Major Religions:	Eastern Orthodox 80%, Sunni Muslim
Annual Income:	$1,840
Urban Population:	67%
Infant Mortality:	15.5 per 1,000
Life Expectancy:	Females 76 yrs, males 70 yrs
Adult Literacy:	Females 97%, males 99%
Health Care:	During the 1990's Bulgaria began allowing free choice of a family doctor. They began accepting money and medicine from Western countries. This began a shift toward private as well as public health care.

_____

References:
Encyclopedic World Atlas. (1994). NY: Oxford University Press.
The World Almanac and Book of Facts 1996. (1995). Mahwah, NJ: World Almanac Books.
G. Curtis, "Bulgaria: A Country Study," Federal Research Division: Library of Congress, 1993.

Sexual   Activity

* Over the last three years the percentage of teen girls under the age of 16 who gave birth was 2.7%. This is higher than the U.S., Poland and Soviet Union, thus indicating the early engagement in sexual activity.[1]
* The age of consent for heterosexual sex is 14 years old.[2]

Contraception

* There are an abundance of contraceptives that are now available in Bulgaria.[3]
* Contraceptives in Bulgaria are not offered to teenagers, students, or socially deprived women at a reduced rate or free.[3]
* There is little opposition from the Orthodox Church regarding the use of contraception and there are adequate supplies on the market, but the lack of use stems from the high price.[1]
* An abortion costs the same as one cycle of contraceptive pills.[1]
* The only emergency contraceptive available in Bulgaria is Postinor; this is a four pill package given to women who do not have sexual intercourse on a regular basis.[4]

Abortion[3]

* The voluntary abortion rate in Bulgaria is one of the highest in Europe, only falling behind the Soviet Union and Romania.
* According to the law of 1956 every woman has a right to an abortion. This was updated in 1992 allowing abortions up to the 12th week of pregnancy. After the 12th week they would be allowed for a medical condition.
* High abortion rates are due to lack of sex education and unavailability of contraceptives.
* From 1985 to 1994 the price of abortions has increased from 2.6 to 21.7% of an average monthly income.
* An abortion in 1993 cost about one week's salary.
* The religion in Bulgaria which is Eastern Orthodox does not oppose the woman's right to voluntary abortions as other religions in Europe do.

Sex Education[1]

* There is a great lack in sex education which is leading to an increase in teenage pregnancy.
* The democratization of the press in Bulgaria led to an explosion of cheap pornographic literature. This in part filled the gap created by a lack of sex education.
* There is little opposition from the Orthodox Church regarding sex education or birth control.

STDs, including AIDS[5]

* As of March 1990 seven cases of AIDS were reported in Bulgaria.
* The infection rate is 34.6 per 1 million people tested or 9.23 per 1 million of the population.
* The sexual ratio of infected people is 3:1 (66 men and 23 women), with 70% aged between 20 and 39 years of age.
* AIDS appeared in Bulgaria in 1987.
* Since August 1987 all donor blood is subject to testing.
* All foreign citizens who enter Bulgaria for more than 3 months must undergo obligatory testing.

Homosexuality

* Gay sex is legal in Bulgaria.[5]
* The age of consent for homosexual and lesbian sex is 14 years old in Bulgaria.[5]
* Gay sex is not allowed in the military in Bulgaria.[2]
* Homosexuality is becoming a target for censorship in Bulgaria, as part of a new government campaign for morality in television.[6]
* On July 25th 1995, Ivan Granitshi, chief of the Bulgarian State Television said that programs featuring homosexuality will be taken off the air.[2]

Prostitution

* Prostitution is now still illegal in Bulgaria, and television shows propagating prostitution are being removed from the air.[6]
* On January 18, 1955 Bulgaria acceded to the Convention for the Suppression of the Traffic in Persons and the Exploitation of the Prostitution of Others. This was a law against prostitution which was

adopted by the 4th session of the General Assembly of the United Nations on December 2, 1949.[7]

Pornography

* No information is available.

Resources

*Bulgarian FPA, 67 Dondukov Bvd. Sofia 1504.
*Bulgarian Medical Academy Coordinating Board of Sexology, P.O. Box 60, Sofia 1431.
*Society for Planned Parenthood and Family Development, Zdrave Street, No. 2, BG-
   1431 Sofia, Bulgaria.

References

1. Goranov, M. & Backardjiev, G. (1993). Teenage pregnancy in Bulgaria, Planned
   Parenthood in Europe, 22 : pg. 16.

2. Wockner, R. "European Laws on Gay Sex Vary",
   http://www.qrd.org/qrd/world/wockner/news. briefs/035-12.31.94 (Updated:
   January 1995).

3. Chernev, T. Hadjiev, C. & Stamenkova, R. (1994). The cost of family planning and
   abortion in Bulgaria, Planned Parenthood in Europe, 23: 12-13.

4. Cherneve,T., Ivanov, S., Dikov, I., & Stamenkova, R. (1995). Prospective study of
   contraception with Levonorgestrel, Planned Parenthood in Europe, Vol. 24, No. 2.

5. Angulov, Z. (1990). AIDS in Bulgaria: A concise overview. Planned Parenthood in
   Europe, Vol. 19, No. 1.

6. Friedman, C. "This Way Out",
   http://www.qrd.org/qrd/media/radio/thiswayout/summary/newswrap/1995/383
   -07.31.95.

7. http://www.un.org/depts/treaty/bible/part-1-E/v11-11.html.

CANADA
POPULATION: 28.5 MILLION

Capital:
Ottawa
(population: 800,000)

Major Cities & Populations: Toronto 3.5 million; Montreal 3 million; Vancouver 1.4 million; Ottawa-Hull 800,000; Edmonton 750,000

Ethnic Groups: British 40%; French 27%; other European 20%; Asiatic 2%; Amerindian/Inuit 2%

Languages: English 63% and French 25% (both official)

Major Religions: Roman Catholic 47%; Protestant 41% Eastern Orthodox, Jewish, Muslim, Hindu

Annual Income per Person: $21,260

Urban Population: 76%

Infant Mortality: 7 per 1,000 births

Life Expectancy: Female 81 years; male 74 years

Adult Literacy: 96%

Health Care System: National health care system

References:
Encyclopedic World Atlas (1994) NY: Oxford University Press.
The World Almanac and Book of Facts 1996 (1995) Mahwah, NJ: World Almanac Books

Sexual   Activity

* One in five 14 year olds and one in two 16 year olds said they had had sexual intercourse at least once.[2]
* Half of Canadian students are sexually active by Grade 11.[3]

Contraception

* Those communities in Ontario where teenagers have access to clinical services for contraception along with sexuality education have lower rates of teen pregnancy.[3]
* According to the Ortho-McNeil survey, the most popular method of birth control for adolescent women is the Pill (22%), used either on its own (9%) or with a condom (13%). Only 5% are not using any form of birth control.[4]
* Parental notification: The age at which it is throught that a person is capable of making his/her own decisions (age of consent) varies among the provinces from 14 to 18 years of age.[5]
* Emergency contraception is available.[6]

Abortion

* More than 70,000 pregnancies, or about 19% of all known pregnancies are terminated annually in Canada. Two-thirds occur among young, single women.[7]
* Almost 90% of abortions are performed in the first trimester (first 12 weeks) of pregnancy.[7]
* Legislation: Legal throughout pregnancy.[8]
* The major issue involving abortion in Canada is access. Access is limited by geography and by attitudes of a minority.[9]
* Cost: Hospital abortions are covered by the national health system; clinic abortions are paid for in some provinces.[10]
* RU-486 is not available in Canada.[9]

Sex   Education

* In most provinces, the law permits each regional school board to set its own guidelines.[11]
* Studies such as the Canada Youth & AIDS Study, which found that most teens are sexually active and most do not use condoms, prompted

schools to improve their sexuality education programs as well as to install condom vending machines in secondary schools.[12]

* Sex education has long been a divisive ethical issue in Canada.[13]

STDs, including AIDS

* Sixty-seven percent of young women surveyed said they practised "safer sex" the first time they had intercourse.[4]
* Cases of STDs in 1993: 13,822 cases of gonorrhea; 3,001 cases of Hepatitis B; 1,444 cases of syphilis.[14]
* AIDS cases as of December 1993: 9,914.[15]

Homosexuality

* The Federal Legislature passed Bill C-33 which added the words "sexual orientation" to its Human Rights Act, which already bans discrimination on the basis of age, gender, race, religion and disability.[16]
* Canada lifted their ban on gays in the miliary in October 1992 after a lesbian lieutenent sued the miliary for discrimination. [17]
* Canada does not recognize gay marriage, although this has been an issue in recent legislation. For example, a same-sex spouse bill was introduced in 1994, but was defeated.[18]

Prostitution[19]

* Prostitution is legal; pimping and operating or being found in or working in a "bawdy house" are not. Solicitation in public is also illegal.

Pornography

* The Canadian criminal law provides that any publication that has as a "dominant characteristic" the "undue exploitation of sex" is obscene. Offenders are usually fined rather than jailed, and the law does not cover those who keep such material for personal use.[20]
* In *Butler v Her Majesty the Queen* (1992) involving the owner of a Manitoba sex shop, the court ruled that although the obscenity law infringed on freedom of expression, it was legitimate to outlaw pornography that was harmful to women. The court also redefined

obscenity as sexually explicit material that involves violence or degradation.[21]

* Criminal code 163.1 makes it illegal to possess, produce, distribute or import child pornography (this includes depictions of youths under 18 and those who look as though they are under 18).[22]

Resources

*Planned Parenthood Federation of Canada, 1 Nicholas Street, Suite 430, Ottawa, Canada K1.
*Sex Information and Education Council of Cananda (SEICAN), 850 Coxwell Avenue, East York, Ontario M4C 5RI Cananda

References

1. Health and Welfare Canada, Report on Adolescent Reproductive Health (Ottawa, 1990).
2. "Sex Life in Canada: A Finding of Increased Activity." Maclean's (Jan 2, 1989), v102, p. 30.
3. L. Hanvey, Facts on Teenage Pregnancy (Planned Parenthood of Cananda, August 1993).
4. D. Mills, Canadian Teenagers Say They Can Wait (Ortho-McNeil Inc., November 1992)
5. H. Rodman & J. Trost, The Adolescent Dilemma (NY: Praeger, 1986), p.27.
6. C. Ellertson et al, "Expanding Access to Emergency Contraception in Developing Countries," Family Planning Perspectives (1995), vol. 26(5), p. 251-263.
7. P. Sachdev, Sex, Abortion & Unmarried Women (Westport, CT: Greenwood, 1993) p. 1, 31.
8. United Nations, Abortion Policies and Procedures: A Global Review (New York, 1993) p. 73.
9. Statistics on Sexuality in Canada, http://www.ncf.carletn.ca/freenet/rootdir/ menus/socialservices/ppo/info/sexstat/sex/stats3.txt (retrieved June 17, 1996).
10. G. Kelley, Sexuality Today (Guilford, CT: Brown & Benchmark, 1995) p. 327.
11. J. Bennett, "Hard Facts for Children," Maclean's (Jan 12, 1987), v100, p.38.
12. D. Kerr, "Condom Vending Machines in Canada's Secondary Schools," Journal of School Health (1990), v60(3), p. 114-115.
13. J. Bennett, "Hard Facts for Children," Maclean's (Jan 12, 1987), v100, p.38.
14. Statistics Canada, Canadian Year Book 1994 (Ottawa, 1993) p. 150.
15. United Nations, Statistical Yearbook (New York, 1995) p. 93.
16. Contemporary Sexuality (published by AASECT), June 1996, vol. 30, no. 6 p. 6.
17. L. Fisher, "Armed and gay," Maclean's (May 24, 1993) v. 106 (21), p. 14.
18. D. Jenish, "A Clash of Violence: Ontario's NDP Meets Resistence as it Tries to Expand Gay Rights." Maclean's (June 13, 1994), v107, p. 10.
19. The World Sex Guide. Last update 1996/04/30. (c) 1194, 1995, 1996. Atta and M. <an48932@anon.penet.fi> (retrieved June 17, 1996).
20. T. Lewin, "Canada Says Pornography Harms Women and Can Be Barred," The New York Times (Feb. 28, 1992), v141, p.B7.
21. Facts on File (March 12, 1992), v52, n2677, p. 176.
22. gopher://gopher.eff.org/00/caf/law/child-porn.can (retreived June 17, 1996).

CHILE
POPULATION: 14 MILLION

Capital:
Santiago
(population: 4.6 million)

Major Cities & Population: Santiago 4.6 million; Concepcion 394,000; Vinademeyer 316,000

Ethnic Groups: Mestizo 92%; Amerindian 7%; Other 1%

Languages: Spanish

Major Religions: Roman Catholic 88%; Protestant 11%

Annual Income per Person: $2,160

Urban Population: 85%

Infant Mortality: 14 per 1,000

Life Expectancy: Females 78 years; Males 72 years

Adult Literacy: 92%

Health Care System: Private Physicians 1 per 889; health care is government responsibility

---

References:
Encyclopedic World Atlas (1994) NY: Oxford University Press.
The World Almanac and Book of Facts 1996 (1995) Mahwah, NJ: World Almanac Books.

Sexual Activity[1]

* Typical age of first intercourse: 18 years old.
* 35% of all females, and 65% of all males have had premarital intercourse.
* 70% of first births are conceived out-of-wedlock.

Contraception[2]

* Most common methods of contraception for females: Pill (25%), Rhythm (15%), IUD (10%); Males: Rhythm (16%), Condom (9%), Withdrawal (8%).
* 20% of females and 19% of males use contraception at first intercourse.
* The percentage of premarital contraception is higher among women 15-19 than 20-24.
* Government has direct support of Emergency Contraception, and it is only available in emergencies.

Abortion

* There are no grounds for abortion.[3]
* Abortion is a criminal offense, in 1989 the government made a law which prohibits abortion (Law No. 18,826).[3]
* Anyone who performs an abortion may receive 3 years in prison.[3]
* Any woman inducing her own miscarriage may go to prison for 5 years.[3]
* During 1990 there were 29 legally performed abortions in Chile. The highest age group was 25-29 year olds, with 14 abortions, followed by 30-34 year olds with 6 abortions.[4]

Sex Education[1]

* There are family planning services, and government supported programs, but since 1980 they have been less vocal in educating.
* There is a lack of appropriate and sufficient sex education in schools.
* Sex isn't a subject that's talked about between family members, or in schools.

STDs, including AIDS

* There were 920 cases of AIDS reported as of December 1993.[5]
* People with AIDS are discriminated against.[6]
* There are support groups for people with AIDS: Chilean AIDS Prevention Council.[6]

Homosexuality[6]

* Homosexuality is illegal. The law is stated in Article 365 of the Chilean Penal Code.
* The International Lesbian and Gay Association is currently working to change this law.

Prostitution[7]

* Prostitution is illegal in all parts of the country.

Pornography

* No information available.

Resources

*Asociacion Chilena de Proteccion de la Familia (APROFA), Avenida Santa Maria 0494, Casukka 16504, Correo 9, Santiago, Chile.

*International Planned Parenthood Federation-Western Hemisphere Region (IPPF/WHR), 902 Broadway, tenth floor, New York, NY 10010.

*Latin American Population Program, Centro de Estudios de Poblacion (CENEP) Casilla 4398, Correo Central, 1000 Buenos Aires

References

1. J. Hearld, M. Valenzuela, & L. Morris, "Premarital Sexual Activity and Contraceptive Use in Santiago, Chile," Studies in Family Planning (March/April 1992), 23(2), p. 128-136.

2. United Nations, Abortion Policies: A Global Review (New York, 1992), p. 82-83.

3. Internet "Sex Education", http://ww.biostat.uscf.edu/caps web/projects/isindex.html (retrieved June 21,1996)

4. L. Schmittroth (1995). Statistical Record of Women Worldwide. New York, NY: Gale Research. p. 614, Table 642.

5. United Nations, Statistical Yearbook (New York, 1995), p. 94.

6. Internet "Action Alert: Hiv discrimination in Chile", http.//www. americas/chile/arlert. hiv.discrimination-01.96 (retrieved June 24, 1996)

7. Internet "Prostitution"http://www.paronia.com/faq/prostitution/santiago. txt.html (retrieved June 19, 1996)

CHINA
POPULATION: 1.2 BILLION

Capital:
Beijing
(population: 9,750,000)

Major Cities & Populations:	Shanghai 12.3 million; Peking (Beijing) 9.75 million, Tianjin 5.45 million
Ethnic Groups:	Han (Chinese) 93%, 55 others
Languages:	Mandarin Chinese (official); in the south and west, local dialects are spoken
Major Religions:	Confucian (officially atheist) 20%; Buddhist 6%; Taoist 2%; Muslim 2%
Annual Income per Person:	$370
Urban Population:	28%
Infant Mortality:	52 per 1,000 live births
Life Expectancy:	Female 69 years; male 67 years
Adult Literacy:	69%
Health Care System:	Three-tier network, made up of county hospitals, township health centers and village health stations, Barefoot Doctors program; 1 doctor for 648 people.

References:
Encyclopedic World Atlas (1994) NY: Oxford University Press.
The World Almanac and Book of Facts 1996 (1995) Mahwah, NJ: World Almanac Books
Women of the World "China: Health" http://www.echonyc.com/~jmkm/wotw/china. health.html, 6/11/96

Sexual Activity

* China places a high value on female virginity. It is an important social norm, which controls the behavior of women.[1]
* Women are regarded as possessions, sex objects, and reproductive tools; in a society such as this sex becomes a commodity.[1]
* China denounces premarital sex,[1] but sexual activity prior to marriage is becoming more common.[2]
* Sexual activity between men and women not involving intercourse is widely practiced and accepted.[2]
* Sex was primarily seen for procreation, but women are now looking for sexual fulfillment and pleasure from sex.[3]
* Chinese population lacks knowledge about sex in general and about women's sexual needs.[4]
* Women are taught that men initiate sex.[3]
* Sexual dissatisfaction is a major cause of China's growing divorce rate.[3]
* Lack of privacy is one reason for sexual repression. Only 13% of married couples have ever made love in the nude.[5]
* Older generations see sexual freedom as a threat to social stability.[3]

Contraception

* In 1979 China established a one-child family policy.[6]
* Contraceptives are usually provided free of charge.[7]
* IUD, tubectomies, vasectomies and induced abortions are considered birth control.[7]
* Oral contraceptives and condoms are also used very infrequently, although they both can be purchased over the counter.[8]
* Contraception is still seen only as family planning and not STD prevention.[8]
* In 1990 more than 85% of women of reproductive age used some form of contraception, yet the rate of contraceptive failure is quite high.[6]

Abortion

* The drug RU486 was approved for use in September, 1988.[7]
* Available on demand, national laws neither criminalize or restrict the procedure.[7]
* Official number of abortions performed annually in China is 10 million.[9]
* China's new law on Maternal and Infant Health Care requires expectant mothers to undergo prenatal exams and to abort any fetus that shows

abnormalities. Because these children neither maintain the family line nor support aging parents, they are considered a "luxury."[10]
* Doctors are permitted to veto the birth of any fetus they find abnormal or prone to genetic disease.[10]
* China forbids couples carrying a serious genetic disease to have children under the new family law.[11]
* They may also veto a marriage if they find either partner genetically unfit.[10]
* 70% of all abortions performed are due to contraceptive failure.[6]
* Approximately 30% of all abortions performed in China are done on unmarried, young females.[8]

Sex Education

* China's first course in sex education started in 1988 at the Peoples' University.[3]
* There is virtually no formal or institutional sex education in China, so young people depend on folklore and each other to learn about sexual matters.[12]
* People still rely on pornography and approved marriage manuals for sex information.[3]
* The population at large does not have enough information to understand transmission behaviors and prevent HIV from spreading.[13]

STDs, including AIDS

* In 1964 China declared itself free of venereal diseases, and research institutes for venereal diseases were closed.[12]
* In 1990, research institutes on venereal diseases were reopened.[12]
* In 1995, 8 major veneral diseases, including HIV, gonorrhea, and syphilis increased to 362,000 cases. By the year 2,000 venereal diseases could become China's leading infectious disease.[14]
* Spread of venereal disease is closely related to prostitution and the public security and health departments have begun forced medical checks of known prostitutes and Johns.[12]
* The consistent effort to eliminate prostitution has halted the spread of venereal disease.[12]
* First HIV seropositive person was identified in 1984 (a non-Chinese foreigner).[8]
* In 1985 four Chinese hemophiliacs (treated with Factor VIII produced in the U.S.) were found to be HIV positive.[8]

* On January 6, 1988 the first case of HIV from sexual transmission was discovered in a Chinese male, homosexual, who acknowledged having sexual contact with foreigners in 1987.[8]
* 2,600 reported HIV, and 80 known AIDS cases.[15]
* Three-quarters of all known AIDS cases are located in the Yunnan province[16] where opium poppies are grown for local consumption and refined heroin passes through in route to port cities in southeastern China.[8]
* AIDS is "nature's punishment" for "unnatural" acts.[3]
* It is estimated that one-half to two-thirds of all STDs occur among the single population.[8]
* Since 1977 to present, 1.3 million cases of STDs have been reported.[7]
* Several national laws require the isolation of individuals while undergoing medical treatment for STD's such as gonorrhea, syphilis and HIV/AIDS.[7]
* Although not officially quarantined, HIV positive individuals and those with AIDS are carefully supervised and regulated.[13]

Homosexuality

* Homosexuality in China can be traced back to reliable sources in the Eastern Zhou dynasty (722-221 B.C.).[17]
* Homosexuality appears to have been part of the sex lives of the rulers of many states of that era.[18]
* Before the 1900's the dominant social construction for males in China was bisexual.[17]
* Political, ritual and social importance of the family unit made procreation a necessity, so bisexuality became more accepted than exclusive homosexuality.[17]
* Homosexual relationships continued up through the 20th century when western influence changed many aspects of China, including homosexuality.[18]
* China shifted from tolerance of same-sex love to open hostility towards homosexuality.[18]
* Homosexuality is looked upon as immoral and punished by "reeducation" in labor camps; fear of discovery and lack of privacy tend to limit the quality and duration of relationships.[17]
* Lesbianism and homosexuality are seen as unrelated and much of the information on male homosexuality does not apply to females.[17]
* Lesbianism, like homosexuality, is seen as a sickness, and patients should receive sympathy and help.[3]

* The "Golden Orchid Association" was an exclusive female membership group. Within this group female couples could marry, with one partner designated as the "husband" and the other the "wife."[17]

Prostitution[19]

* In 1991 prostitution was prohibited in China.
* Forced re-education is punishment for prostitutes and Johns, which includes legal and moral education and manual labor in a specified camp. Time spent in these camps ranges from half a year to two years.

Pornography

* In November 1989 a campaign against pornographic activities and publications was introduced.[20] Because of harmful effects on society the campaign won universal support.[21]
* The resolution of pornography stipulates the death penalty or life imprisonment for serious cases of smuggling, producing, selling or distribution pornographic materials.[22]
* Belief that pornography is poison and it is changing the lives of young adults; studies show that students who view pornographic material slacken in their academic efforts and have less desire to be successful.[20] Pornographic materials are not available to people under 18, and is strictly punished.[22]
* Reference to homosexuality was deleted in new translations of Chinese classical literature. Chinese could no longer read the classics in uncensored form.[22]
* Books on anatomy and literary and art works containing sexually explicit material will not be considered pornographic materials.[18]

Resources

*China Association of Sex Education, Mercy Memorial Foundation, 11F, 171 Roosevelt Road, Section 3, Taipei Taiwan, R.O.C.

*China Family Planning Association, 1 Bei Li, Shengguzhuang, He Ping Li, Beijing.

*China Sexology Association, Number 38, Xue Yuan Lu, Haidion, Beijing 1000083.

*State Family Planning Commission, IEC Dept., 14 Zhichun Road, Haidian District, Beijing 100088.

References

1. X. Zhou, (1989 Summer). Virginity and premarital sex in contemporary China, Feminist Studies, 15 (n2), pp. 279-288.
2. G. Kelly, Sexuality Today (Guilford, CT: Brown & Benchmark, 1995) p. 33
3. L. Jaivin, (1991, Jan 10). Sex Attitudes in China for the '90s, The Wall Street Journal, p. A12.
4. S. Faison, (1995, Aug. 22). In China, rapid social changes bring a surge in the divorce rate, New York Times, pA1.
5. China's sexual revolution, Contemporary Sexuality, (May 1993) 25 (n5), pp. 2-3.
6. United Nations, Abortion Policy: A Global Review, (New York, 1992) pp. 84-86.
7. Women of the World, China: Contraception and Contraceptive Technology http://www.echonyc.com/~jmkm/wotw/china.contraception.html. (6/17/96).
8. V. E. Gil, (1991, November). An ethnography of HIV/AIDS and sexuality in the People's Republic of China, The Journal of Sex Research, Vol. 28 (n4), pp. 521-537.
9. L. Schmittroth (1995). Statistical Record of Women Worldwide. New York, NY: Gale Research, p. 614, Table 642.
10. AASECT, (1995, March). Chinese eugenics law to limit disabled births, Contemporary Sexuality, 29 (n3), p. 9.
11. AASECT, (1994, Dec). China bans sex-screening of fetuses. Contemporary Sexuality, 28 (n12), p. 14.
12. Y. Xiaobing, (1991, Dec. 16). China launches anti-prostitution campaign, Beijing Review Vol. 34 (n50), pp. 27-29.
13. V. E. Gil, (1994), Sinic conundrum: A history of HIV/AIDS in the People's Republic of China, The Journal of Sex Research, Vol. 31 (n3), pp. 211-217.
14. C. Henderson (1996). China venereal disease rates rising 18% annually. AIDS Weekly Plus, p. 19.
15. G. Cowley, (1996, April 1). From freedom to fear: When AIDS hits China, Newsweek, Vol. 127 (n14), p. 49.
16. (1996, April 17). China to define quarantine zone. Boston Globe Vol. 249, p. 17
17. W. Dynes, Encyclopedia of Homosexuality (NY: Garland Pub. 1980), pp. 215-220.
18. B. Hinsch, Passions of the cut sleeve: The male homosexual tradition in China (Berkeley: University of California Press, 1990), pp. xvii-232.
19 Y. Xiaobing, (1991, Dec. 16). China launches anti-prostitution campaign, Beijing Review Vol. 34 (n50), pp. 27-29.
20. C. Gang, (1990, March 19). China declares war on pornography, Beijing Review Vol. 33 (n12), pp. 26-29.
21. Lili, C., (1989, October 16). Discard the dross, make literature and art prosper, Beijing Review, 32 (n42), p. 7.
22. (1991, January 14). NPC enacts laws on drugs, pornography, Beijing Review, 34 (n2), p. 7.

COSTA RICA
POPULATION: 3.5 MILLION

Capital:
San Jose
(population: 318,765)

Major Cities & Populations: San Jose 318,765; Alajuela 171,840; Cartago 118,205

Ethnic Groups: White (including mestizo) 96%; Black 2%; Indian 1%; Chinese 1%

Languages: Spanish (official); English

Major Religions: Roman Catholic 95%

Annual Income Per Person: $5,050

Urban Population: 48%

Infant Mortality: 10 per 1000 births

Life Expectancy: Female 80 years; Male 76 years

Adult Literacy: 93%

Health Care: There are 885 doctors, 275 dentists, 245 pharmacists and 453 nurses per 1 million people. There are 3 hospital beds per 1,000 people. 80% of the population has access to health services. Only 54% of the population has access to prenatal care.

References:
Encyclopedic World Atlas (1994) NY: Oxford University Press.
Europa World Year Book 1996 (1995) London: Europa Publications Limited.
The World Almanac and Book of Facts 1996 (1995) Mahwah, NJ: World Almanac Books

Sexual Activity[1]

* 59% of unmarried women ages 15-24 who became pregnant reported that the pregnancy was unintended.

Contraception[2]

* 70% of women use some form of contraception.

Abortion[3]

* Abortion is legal only when maternal health is compromised.

Sex Education

* No information available.

STD's including AIDS[4]

* As of 9/30/95, there were 851 cases of AIDS in Costa Rica.
* It is estimated that 9,000 individuals are HIV+ in Costa Rica.

Homosexuality[5]

* Homosexuality is not acceptable in Costa Rica; there is a lot of discrimination against gays and lesbians.

Prostitution[6]

* Prostitution is legal in Costa Rica.
* Prostitutes must have an ID card and carry it at all times to prove it.
* Age of consent is 18.

Pornography

* No information available.

Resources

*Asociacion Demografica Costarricense (ADC), La Uruca 300 metros al Norte y 100, metros al Este de la Fabrica de Galletas Pozoluelo, Apartado Postal 10203, San Jose, Costa Rica.

*Programa Salud Reproductiva, Apartado 1434-1011 Y-Griega, San Jose, Costa Rica.

References

1. Population Reports, Vol. 23. N.3, Oct. (1995). pg. 3-11.

2. The Economist Book of World Vital Statistics. (1990). Times Books.

3. Sexuality and Gender in Society. (1990). Harper Collins Publishers, pg. 452.

4. World Health Organization: The Current Global Situation of the HIV/AIDS Pandemic. Dec. (1995).

5. http://www/qrd.org/qrd/world/americas/costa   rica

6. The World Sex Guide. Last updated: 1996/04/30. (C) 1994, 1995, 1996 Atta and M. <an48932@anon.penet.fi>. (retreived June 26, 1996).

CUBA
POPULATION: 10.5 MILLION

Capital:
Havana
(population: 2 million)

Major Cities & Populations: Havana 2 million; Santiago 380,000; Camaguey 275,00

Ethnic Groups: Mulatto 51%; White 37%; Black 11%; Chinese 1%

Languages: Spanish (offical)

Major Religions: Roman Catholic 40%; Protestant 3%

Annual Income per Person: $3,000

Urban Population: 74%

Infant Mortality: 8 per 1,000 births

Life Expectancy: Females 79 years; Males 75 years

Adult Literacy: 91%

Health Care System: 1 doctor per 677; 1 bed per 134

References:
Encyclopedic World Atlas (1994) NY: Oxford University Press.
The World Almanac and Book of Facts (1995) Mahwah, NJ: World Almanac Books
"Cuba " The CIA Factbook, http://www.odcl.gov/cia/publications/95fact/ch.html
(retrieved June 10, 1996)

Sexual   Activity

* No information available.

Contraception

* Contraception is widely available in Cuba in all government health centers, but contraception failure is high.[1]
* It is estimated that approximately 70 per cent of Cuban women of reproductive age are currently using a contraceptive method.[1]
* Cuba needs 160 million condoms a year, but can only afford 43 million.[2]

Abortion[1]

* Abortion has been legal in Cuba since the late 1960s.
* The pregnant woman must be examined by a gynacologist and must receive counseling from a social worker.
* If the woman is unmarried and under 16 years of age, parental permission is required.
* If gestation is greater than 10 weeks, authorization by health authorities is required.
* The abortion must be performed by a physician in an official health center.

Sex   Education

*No information available.

STDS, Including AIDS

* Cuba is the only country that imposes AIDS test on all its people, and the only one that confines for life anyone carrying the HIV virus.[3]
* Cuba established an extensive HIV surveillance program in 1983, and more than 15 million HIV antibody test have been done.   The sexual contacts of all infected persons are closely observed.[3]
* Cuba has one of the lowest HIV-infection rates in the world: only 7.3 cases per 1 million people, compared to the United States rate of 241 cases per 1 million.[4]
* Cuba has reported 1,600 HIV-positive patients and 400 AIDS deaths.[2]

Homosexuality[5]

* A 1965 Ministry of Health report concluded that there were no known biological causes of homosexuality; no genetic and hormonal causes and no effective biological treatment.
* Homosexual behavior in the public sphere is illegal; there were 3-9 month fines for anyone who practices homosexual acts or makes public displays of homosexuality.
* Today life for gay people in Cuba is similar, in some sense, to life for gay people in the United States, however the homosexuality of many men and women is a matter of public record. It is the complete abscence of a public sphere that most clearly distinguishes the life of homosexuals in Cuba from any corresponding lifestyle in the United States.

Prostitution

* Prostitution is still illegal in Cuba, however the 40% rise in tourism in Cuba over the past two years has spawned a resurgence of the nation's sex industry.[4]
* Customers are not prosecuted.[6]

Pornography

* No information available.

Resources

*Centro Iberoamericano de Formacano Pedagogica y Orintacion Educational (CIFPOE), Calle 108. Number 29E08, entre 29 E y 29 F, Ciudad Escolar Libertad, Mariano, La Habana.
*Sociedad Cinetifica Cubana Para el Desarrollo de la Familia(SOCUDEF), 5ta Avenida 3207, Esquina 34, Miramar, Havana, Cuba

References

1. United Nations, <u>Abortion Policies: A Global Review,</u> (NY. 1992) pp. 97-98.

2. "Cuban Hookers Rounded up at Imfamous Resort." <u>Knight-Rider Newspaper</u>, June 7, 1996.

3. Dynes,W.,<u>Encyclopedia of Homosexuality Vol.1 A-index,</u> (NY: Garland Publishing Inc., 1990), pp.285-87.

4. "Prostitution soars as tourists return to Cuba," <u>Contemporary Sexuality</u> (published by AASECT, November,1995) 29(11) .pp.8.

5. Leiner,M., <u>Sexual Politics In Cuba: Machism, Homosexuality, and AIDS</u>(CA 1994)pp.21-47.

6. <u>The World Sex Guide.</u> Last update 1996/04/30. (c) 1994,1995,1996 Atta and M. <u><an48932@anon.penet.fi></u>

CZECH REPUBLIC
POPULATION: 10.3 MILLION

Capital:
Prague (Praha)
(population: 1.2 million)

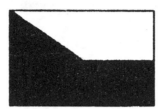

Major Cities & Populations:	Brno 400,000; Ostrava 330,000; Pilsen 170,000
Ethnic Groups:	94% Czech, 3% Slovak, Polish, Gypsy
Languages:	Czech (official), German, Russian, English
Major Religions:	Atheism 39.8%, Roman Catholic 39.2%
Income Per Capita:	$7,350
Urban Population:	75%
Infant Mortality:	9 per 1000 births
Life Expectancy:	Females 77 years, Males 70 years
Adult Literacy:	100%
Health Care System:	Private practice encouraged, good insurance system, all activities directed by the Minister of Health, with attention to preventive medicine.

References:
Worldmark Encyclopedia of the Nations: Europe, Vol. 5, Eighth Edition, pp. 99-106,
        Gale Research Inc, Detroit, 1995.
The World Almanac and Book of Facts 1996 (1995), Mahwah, NJ: World Almanac Books
CIA World Factbook, 1995, <http://www.odci.gov//cia/publications/95fact/ez.html>.

Sexual   Activity[1]

* Age of consent for sexual activity is 15.[1]
* Since 1989 the Czech Republic has been experiencing a sexual revolution, development of a sex industry, and societal tendencies toward increased sexual activity.[2]

Contraception

* Until 1990, condoms were the only contraceptives that had to be paid for. However, the use of contraception was very low, with only 7.2 percent of women aged 15-44 using the pill, and only 16.9 percent using an IUD.[3]
* Until 1990, women were told that oral contraceptives and IUDs were hazardous to their health, and thus relied on abortions as birth control.[4]
* Today, only 28% of women at risk of unplanned pregnancy use modern contraceptives.[4]
* Under the new economic policy, consumers must pay for abortion and contraceptive supplies.[4]
* IUD insertion is covered by health insurance.[4]
* Oral contraceptives cost only 1-2% of an average monthly income.
* Since 1990, when women first had to pay for contraception, modern contraceptive method use has been *increasing*, according to growing sales of contraceptives.[4]
* Gynecologists view condoms as somewhat convenient, and only somewhat reliable against pregnancy and disease.[4]
* Only 65% of gynecologists think that abstinence is 100% reliable against unplanned pregnancy and sexually transmitted disease, and only 39% of them perceived this as a 'very safe' method. 5% viewed it as a convenient method.[4]
* 80% of gynecologists prescribe the Pill very often. amd 63% of them view it as 100% reliable, while only 25% of them perceive it to be 'very safe.' 90% believe that the Pill is very convenient.[4]
* Postinor, a post-coital contraceptive or "morning-after" pill, is registered in the Czech Republic.[5]

Abortion

* Abortion is available on request, with the consent of the woman and authorization by her gynecologist. After 12 weeks, abortion may be performed for medical reasons only.[6]

* Except for medical reasons, they must be performed during the first trimester in a hospital, by a licensed gynecologist.[6]
* Women under the age of 16 must have parental/guardian consent, and women between the ages of 16 and 18 must notify their parent/guardian.[6]
* 75% of abortions are performed using the vacuum aspiration method.[6]
* Legislation is becoming more and more liberal.[3]
* Termination of pregnancy for other than health reasons now can cost from 20-50% of the average monthly salary.[3]
* The number of abortions have slowly decreased since 1990's changes to the price system.[3]

Sex Education

* One of the priorities of the Czech Family Planning Association is to make sex education more effective.[3]
* Sex education is mainly taught as a part of biology, health or other science classes.[7]
* Family Life Education is also a specific course subject, where sex education is addressed.[7]
* The Czech Republic begins sex education with gender physical differences and roles. This is taught to younger children. Pre-adolescents are taught reproduction facts, including puberty and hygiene. Adolescents are taught biological facts, contraception, and AIDS and STD prevention.[7]
* The Czech Republic has a preventive model of sex education.[7]
* The Family Planning Association is the main agency involved with sex education. It provides teacher training, youth lectures, and it belongs to a sex education policy-making body, and provides advocacy.[7]
* Public climate towards sex education is moderate.[7]

STDs, including AIDS

* Czechoslovakia has had 84 AIDS cases, primarily in homosexual and bisexual males.[8]
* 50-60% of all new syphilis cases are found in the population group of 15 and 24 years of age. The population this disease was found in earlier was 65 years and older.[2]
* 70% of all gonorrhea cases are found in the population group between 15 and 24 years.[2]

Homosexuality[9]

* SOHO is the Czech abbreviation for their Association of Homosexual Citizen's Organizations, made up of about 20 organizations.
* SOHO representatives have met every three months since 1991.
* The age of consent for homosexuals in the Czech Republic has been reduced to 15 (from 18), the same as for heterosexuals.
* SOHO provides AIDS education.
* Since 1995, SOHO has worked towards official registered homosexual partnerships in the Czech Republic.

Prostitution

* Prostitutes can be found through the magazine *Prag at Night*, which is available at bookstands.[10]
* Prostitutes can be ticketed, but are generally not bothered when talking with a customer.[10]
* July 11, 1990 abolished two penal laws concerning prostitution, since that date it is no longer considered a criminal offense.[2]
* The high earings associated with prostitution have made it an attractive occupation.[2]
* Most prostitutes operate in the streets of large cities or on highways.[2]
* Most prostitutes are less than 18 years of age and many started as young as 13 or 14 years old.[2]

Pornography

* Since the fall of communism in 1989, Czech media lifted its ban on censorship, and pornography began to fluorish.[11]
* Foreign publications, such as *Penthouse* and *Playboy* are popular, as well as those of the Czech Republic.[12]
* Presently, there is no prohibitive government ban on pornography.[11]

Resources

Czech Society for Family Planning & Sex Education, Panska 1, POB 399, 111 21 Praha 1
Czechoslavak Sexological Society/Institute of Sexolody, Charles University, Prague,
   Karlov Nam_sti 32, Prague 2, 120 00.

References

1. Alan F. Reekie, "Age of Consent Laws in the Council of Europe States in 1993,"
   <http://ftp.tcp.com/qrd/world/europe/age.of.consent.laws-12.20.94>.

2. V. Kastanlova (1995). Increasing sexually transmitted disease rates among
   prostitutes in the Czech Republic. Journal of Community Health, 20(2), 219-223.

3. R. Uzel and V. Wynnyczuk, "Private Fee No Barrier to Family Planning in the
   Czech Republic," Planned Parenthood in Europe (1994), Vol. 23, No. 1.

4. A. Visser, R. Uzel, E. Ketting, N. Bruyniks, & B. Oddens, "Practice, Attitudes and
   Knowledge of Czech and Slovak Gynaecologists Concerning Contraception,"
   Planned Parenthood in Europe (1994), Vol. 23, No. 1

5. S. Camp. "A study-tour report on emergency contraception in seven
   European countries." Washington, DC: Reproductive Health Technologies
   Project, 1994.

6. United Nations, Abortion Policies: A Global Review (NY, 1992).

7. D. Vilar, "School Sex Education: Still a Priority in Europe," Planned Parenthood
   in Europe (1994), Vol. 23, No. 3, pp. 8-12.

8. HIV.NET, <http://www.hiv.net>, 6/19/96

9. SOHO Ceska Republika, <http://www.infima.cz/soho/>, 6/12/96.

10. The World Sex Guide, "Prostitution in: Czech Republic,"
    <http://www.paranoia.com/faq/prostitution/Czech-Republic.html> last updated
    4/30/96.

11. C. Carty, "Media Change in the Czech Republic,"
    <http://www.utexas.edu/ftp/pub/eems/czech-republic.html>, last updated
    8/15/94.

12. "Czech Penthouse Launched," CTK National News Wire, 4/12/94

DENMARK
POPULATION: 5 MILLION

Capital:
Copenhagen
(population: 1,346,289)

Major Cities & Populations:	Copenhagen 1,346,289; Arhus 274,535; Odense 181,824; Aalborg 158,141
Ethnic Groups:	97% Danish
Languages:	Danish, Faroese, Greenlandic (an Eskimo dialect), German (small minority).
Major Religions:	91 % Evangelical Lutheran
Annual Income Per Person:	$ 23,660
Urban Population:	85%
Infant Mortality:	6 per 1,000 births
Life Expectancy:	Female 79 years; Male 73 years
Adult Literacy:	99%
Health Care System:	Doctors are appointed by Health Security Service; few private clinics, mostly hospitals.

References:
"Denmark" The CIA Factbook, http://www.odcl.gov/cia/publications/95fact/ch.html (retrieved June 10, 1996)
Encyclopedic World Atlas (1994) NY: Oxford University Press
Roemer, Milton I. (1993) National Health Systems of the World: The Issues. Vol II, Oxford University Press.
The World Almanac and Book of Facts 1996 (1995) Mahwah, NJ World Almanac Books

Sexual   Activity

* Denmark has a very liberal attitude towards teenage sexuality and has recognized the fact that young, unmarried women have a sexual life.[1]
* In 1987, a survey was done of 28 9th grade classes, a total of 438 students, in which 34% had experienced sexual activity and reported to have had sexual intercourse an average of 5 times a month.[2]
* Teenage pregnancies are not too common. The number has been decreasing rapidly for the past 20 years. 12 children were born to mothers under 16 years of age in 1993. Most teenage pregnancies end with an abortion.[1]
* Age of consent is 15 years of age.[3]

Contraception

* In March 1991, the Family Planning Association launched a series of 10 pamphlets on different contraceptive methods which were distributed free of charge.   By 1995, 150,000 copies had been distributed.[4]
* Parental consent is not needed for young people to acquire contraceptives.   Denmark was the first country in the world to grant this right to youth in 1966.[1]
* Teens: In 1987, a survey given to 28 9th grade classes revealed that 90% of the participants wished to be given free condoms. Roughly 40% of pupils had not used a condom during their latest intercourse.[2]
* Emergency contraception: The most popular method of contraception is the morning after pill which is taken with-in 2-3 days of intercourse but is available in a strip of 21 pills only. In 1994, the total sales of the 21 pack was 14,000. In April 1995, the surgeon general ordered that a pack for emergency use should be available on prescription.[4]

Abortion

* In 1993, the annual number of abortions was about 18,500; one of the highest rates in Western Europe.[4]
* Single women & women under age 20 have the highest abortion rates.[5]
* Legislation: Denmark has had free access to legal abortion since 1973 when a law passed that allowed women to have an abortion on demand during the first 12 weeks of pregnancy after the submission of an application and after being informed of the risks and alternatives. Abortion is available after 12 weeks when authorized by a committee of

one social worker and two physicians. They would approve if one of many conditions applied.[5]

* RU 486 (non-surgical "abortion pill"): Not available in Denmark.[4]

Sex Education[1]

* Sex and social life education has been a compulsory subject in Danish schools since 1970 but has been a tradition long before then.
* The sex education curriculum focuses on medical and anatomical lessons, psychological and ethical aspects of sexual and couples' relations, love, sexuality, pregnancy, STD's, and abortion, homosexuality and knowledge about sexual minorities.

STD's, including AIDS

* Despite a nationwide "safe sex" campaign, roughly 40% of pupils in the 9th grade survey had not used a condom during their latest intercourse.[2]
* Reported cases of gonorrhea had decreased in the 1980's.[1]
* As of June 1996, Denmark has 1,928 HIV-positive cases,[6] one of the highest rates in Europe.[7]
* 1 in 6 Danish males have had intercourse with a high-risk partner.[8]
* An AIDS hotline funded by the Danish government has been established.[7]

Homosexuality

* A law passed in 1989 that allows "registered partnership for two persons of the same sex". These ceremonies take place in a town hall, not in a church. These couples are treated legally as "single" people once they leave Denmark's borders.[9]
* Over 1,300 partnerships have been entered into since 1989; 17 of these have since been dissolved.[9]
* Homosexuals are welcome in the armed forces of Denmark.[10]
* Age of consent for gay men and lesbian women is 15 years of age.[3]

Prostitution[1]

* Prostitution is not a criminal offense in Denmark. Neither the customer, nor the prostitute are committing an offense.

* Prostitution is considered criminal vagrancy if the woman has no other means of support.
* The legal age of consent for sex: 15.

Pornography

* A "porno wave" began in Denmark around 1964 but had receded by 1970 after pornography was legalized in the late 1960's.[11]
* Possession of child pornography is a crime since 1994 as well as the sale and production of child pornography.[1]
* Pornographic material is widely available.[12]

Resources

Danish Association for Clinical Sexology (DACS), Kuhlausgade 46, DK-2100, Copenhagen. Phone: 45/392-92399 Fax: 45/354-57684.

The Danish Family Planning Association, Aurehojvej 2, DK-2900, Hellerup. Phone: 45/31-625688 Fax: 45/31-620282.

References

1. "Sexual Rights of Young Women" The Danish Family Planning Association & The Swedish Association for Sex Education (Denmark, 1995) p. 11.

2. S. Kjoller, B. Hansen & E. Segest. "Free Condoms in the Schools of Copenhagen, Denmark" Journal of School Health (Feb 1989) Vol. 59, No. 2, p. 66.

3. Alan F. Reekie, "Age of Consent Laws in the Council of Europe States in 1993," <http://ftp.tcp.com/qrd/world/europe/age.of.consent.laws-12.20.94>.

4. A. Christensen. "Restoring sexual hangovers with few side effects" Planned Parenthood in Europe (Aug 1995) Vol. 24, No. 2, p. 18.

5. United Nations, Abortion Policies: A Global Review (New York, 1992) p. 106.

6. "HIV.NET"   http://www.hiv.net Retrieved 6/19/96.

7. N. Miller. "Out in the World: Gay & Lesbian Life from Buenos Aires to Bangkok" (New York, 1992) p. 347-348.

8. L. Remez. "One in six Danish males have had intercourse with a high-risk partner" Family Planning Perspective (Nov/Dec 1992) Vol. 24, No. 6, p. 280.

9. H. Lyding. "Homosexual 'Marriage' in Scandinavia" Planned Parenthood in Europe (1993) Vol. 22, No. 1, p. 14.

10. R. Wockner. "European laws on gay sex vary" International News (Dec 1994) Internet: rwockner@netcom.com.

11. M. Kimmel. "Men confront pornography" (New York, 1990) p. 233 & 244.

12. G. Kelly. Sexuality Today (Guilford, CT: Brown & Benchmark, 1995) p. 446.

EGYPT
POPULATION: 62 MILLION

Capital:
Cairo
(population: 6 million)

Major Cities & Populations:	Cairo 6.3 million; Alexandria 2.9 million; Giza 1.8 million
Ethnic Groups:	99% Eastern Hamitic (Egyptians, Bedouins and Berbers)
Languages:	Arabic (official), English and French widely understood by educated classes.
Major Religions:	94% Muslim (mostly Sunni)
Annual Income Per Person:	$620
Urban Population:	44%
Infant Mortality:	74 per 1,000 births
Life Expectancy:	Female 63 years; Male 59 years
Adult Literacy:	45%
Health Care System:	Free health service provided by gov't; fee-for-service by private physicians.

References:
"Egypt" The CIA World Fact Book 1995
Encyclopedic World Atlas (1994) NY: Oxford University Press
Roemer, Milton I. (1993) National Health Systems of the World; The Issues. Vol II, Oxford University Press.
The World Almanac and Book of Facts 1996 (1995) Mahwah, NJ World Almanac Books

Sexual Activity[1]

* Interaction between the sexes is extremely limited prior to marriage; marriage is difficult because it is very expensive; it is unacceptable to live together unless married; sexes are extremely segregated.
* Dating is viewed with disapproval in this society where arranged marriages are prevalent.
* Sex with animals is not uncommon.
* Incest is not uncommon.

Contraception

* Egyptian Family Planning Association has been providing services since 1958.[2] Egypt is a leader in family planning in the Middle East, a region where contraceptive use is relatively low.[3]
* Contraceptives are also available through a number of private sector agencies.[2]
* According to a survey done in 1992, of 10,000 households, 30.8% of married women; 29.6% of single women; 5.0% of previously married women were currently using contraception. 34.6% of married women were not using contraception. 27.9% of married women were using IUD's. 12.9% of married women were using the pill.[4]
* More than 90% of Egyptian girls undergo a surgical "female circumcision" to control or prevent sexual intercourse.[5] About 2 million girls per year are subjected to female genital mutilation, largely through parental consent and custom.[6]
* In 1994, the Egyptian government pledged at the U.N. Population Conference to outlaw female circumcision entirely.[7]
* In 1959, the act of performing female circumcision surgery in the state hospitals was banned.[7] In June 1995, the Egyptian Health Minister ordered that state hospitals perform female circumcision surgery one day a week in an effort to stop untrained amateurs from performing the procedure which has not as of this date, been banned.[7]
* Emergency contraception: not yet available.[8]

Abortion

* Abortion in Egypt is illegal.[3] The Egyptian penal code of 1937 prohibits abortion in all circumstances but under criminal law, abortion is permitted to save the life of the pregnant woman; the husband's consent is required.[3]

* Anyone who induces an abortion is subject to imprisonment.[3]
* More recently, different approaches are taken on abortion, ranging from complete prohibition (the Maliki sect) to complete permission (the Zaydi sect). As a result of conflicting legal status and differing theological opinions, the availability of safe abortion services is limited in Egypt.[9]
* RU 486 (non-surgical "abortion pill"): Not available in Egypt.[9]

Sex Education[1]

* Open discussion of sexuality is socially unacceptable; Egypt uses an approach that emphasizes repression rather than education.

STD's, including AIDS

* In Egypt, there appears to be a small amount of AIDS awareness. Aids cases are either rare or covered up; safe sex practices are virtually unknown; sex roles are very rigid; most Egyptian men will not allow themselves to be penetrated by foreigners; As of 1992, there were only a handful of AIDS cases reported.[1]
* In 1992, mandatory HIV testing of all resident foreigners.[1]
* As of 1993, 91 AIDS cases have been reported.[10]

Homosexuality

* Women are off-limits and men are in close physical contact with other men.[1]
* There is a strong social sanction against an openly gay or lesbian life. Homosexuality is taboo but very common (more so among men).[1]
* Men have traditionally had sex with other men until marriage and sometimes after that, but it's discreet. Lesbianism is also common but discreet.[1]
* There are no official gay organizations or gay bars but a few hammams-Turkish baths for men.[1]
* According to a survey done by the United States Department of Defense between 1982 & 1984, Egypt reported having no exclusive military policies regarding homosexual behavior. 12% of Egyptians reported religious disapproval of homosexual behavior; 32% of Egyptians feel that homosexuality is considered a psychiatric problem; 9% of Egyptians reported that the government minimizes the existence of homosexual behavior in the military.[11]

Prostitution

* Data not available.

Pornography[12]

* Censorship: No video or record album may be legally sold until it is scrutinized by a government censor to ensure that the work adhere's to the countries "specific moral standards."

Resources

Alexandria Model Family Planning Clinic, 17, Sidi El-Metwally Street, El-Attarien, Alexandria, 4933867. Phone: 20-3/493-3867.

Egyptian Family Planning Association, 6 Gazirat El Arab Street, Al Mohandissen, El Giza, Cairo. Phone: 20-2/360-7329.

References

1. N. Miller. "Out in the World: Gay and Lesbian life from Buenos Aries to Bangkok" (New York, 1992) p. 78-90.

2. United Nations, Abortion Policies: A Global Review (New York, 1992) p. 118.

3. D. Trottier, L. Potter, B. Taylor, & L. Glover. "Reports: User Characteristics and Oral Contraceptive Compliance in Egypt" Studies in Family Planning (Sept/Oct 1994) Vol. 25, No. 5, p. 284-292.

4. "Data: Egypt 1992: Results from the Demographic and Health Survey" Studies in Family Planning (July/Aug 1994) Vol. 25, No. 4, p. 243-247.

5. B. Crosette. "In Cairo, pleas to stop maiming girls: foes show models of mutilated female genitals" The New York Times (Sept 11 1994) Vol. 143, p. 6(N), col. 4.

6. R. Berhane. "The facts about FGM in Egypt-an overview" WIN News (Autumn 1994) Vol. 20, No. 4, p. 30(1).

7. "Studies in Short: Egyptian Government orders hospitals to perform female circumcision" Contemporary Sexuality (July 1995) Vol. 29, No. 7, p. 9.

8. "Population Reports: Meeting the Needs of Young Adults" Family Planning Programs (Oct 1995) Series J. No. 41, p. 1-5.

9. D. Huntington, E. Hassan, N. Attallah, N. Toubia, M. Naguib, & L. Nawar. "Improving the Medical Care Counseling of Postabortion Patients in Egypt" Studies in Family Planning (Nov/Dec 1995) Vol. 26, No. 6, p. 351.

10. United Nations Statistical Yearbook (New York, 1995) p. 96.

11. S. Harris. "Military Policies Regarding Homosexual Behavior: An International Survey" Journal of Homosexuality (1991) Vol.21, No. 4, p. 67-75.

12. D. Jehl. "Egyptians say Israel is waging a sex war" The New York Times (Oct 10, 1995) Vol. 145, p. A5 (N), p. A4 (L), col. 1.

FINLAND
POPULATION: 5 MILLION

Capital:
Helsinki
(population: 502,000)

Major Cities & Populations:	Espoo 179,000; Tamere 175,000
Ethnic Groups:	Finns 94%; Swedes, Lapps
Languages:	Finnish, Swedish (Both Official)
Major Religions:	Evangelical Lutheran 89%
Annual Income per Person:	$16,100
Urban Population:	64%
Infant Mortality:	5 per 1,000 births
Life Expectancy:	Females 80 years; Males 73 years
Adult Literacy:	100%
Health Care System:	Physicians: 1 per 390 persons

References:
Encyclopedic World Atlas (1994) NY: Oxford University Press.
The World Almanac and Book of Facts 1996 (1995) Mahwah, NJ: World Almanac Books

Sexual   Activity

* The proportion of sexually experienced adolescents aged 15 in 1990 was 29% for girls and 25% for boys.[1]
* There are no signs of increasing sexual activity among adolescents, despite rigorous sex education in the schools and mass media.[1]
* The age of consent is 16 for heterosexual and 18 for homosexual relations.[2]

Contraception

* In 1972 legislation added an entry into force of the Primary Health Care Act. The law ordered that every local municipality must have a health centre which provides primary health care services for its inhabitants, including contraceptive counseling.[1]
* The services are free of charge and in larger cities and communities the services are concentratcd in family planning clinics.[3]
* A visit to the family planning clinic and the first contraceptive method (for instance oral contraceptives for 3-6 months) are free of charge. The services are funded by local municipalities with the support of government subsidies, the most common being the Family Federation of Finland, which has clinics in most of the larger towns of the country and a youth center in Helsinki.[1]
* Adolescents can also resort to school health services, which offer advice in sexual and contraceptive problems.[1]
* Teens: 27% of girls and 20% of boys had not used effective contraceptive methods at their first coitus.[1]
* Oral contraceptive use: 41% of 18 year old girls, 19% among 16 year olds, and 2% for 14 year olds.[1]
* In the 1980s in Finland the IUD and the condom were the main contraceptive methods used. However, the use of the Pill has increased in the last few years.[4]
* Emergency Contraception (also called "postcoital" birth control): Obtained from the family planning centers or a pharmacy with a prescription, and has been available since the mid 1980s. Although use is impossible to estimate, the sales figures of the special post-coital contraception package show an increasing trend.[3]

Abortion

* Legislation: In 1970 passed a much broader law than previously which includes sufficient social grounds for abortion. In 1979 a restriction was included in the law according to which an abortion induced on social grounds must be performed during the first 12 weeks of pregnancy. The law forbids abortion after the 16th week of pregnancy except on medical grounds, in which case there is no limitation, and abortion may be granted up to the 24th week on eugenic grounds.[5]
* It is estimated that the number of illegal abortions in the 1950s and 1960s varied between 18,000 and 25,000 annually. Under present law they have gradually disappeared almost totally.[5]
* An indication that abortion has not become a birth control method in Finland is that the majority of abortions induced annually are first ones.[5]
* Under current law, access to abortions services is fairly equal throughout Finland.[5]
* Minors need consent from parents, and the cost is free of charge if performed in a public hospital.[6]

Sex Education[1]

* The need for more effective sex education among teenagers was recognized at the preparatory stage of the present abortion law, and sex education was integrated into the curriculum in 1970.
* Currently, sex education in Finland begins at age 11 on changes in puberty and advances from there on according to the children's developmental stage. By the age of 16 all adolescents should have learned about both the physiology of reproduction and methods of contraception.
* The Finnish program against HIV has one feature which is probably unique in the world; every year since 1987 the national health authorities have mailed an illustrated magazine to all adolescents who will be 16 that year containing information on the prevention of HIV and other STDs, as well as on sexual issues in general. The package also contains a condom and a letter to the parents. Public response to this campaign has been mainly positive, and it has probably contributed to the increased knowledge of sexual issues among teenagers.

STDs, Including AIDS

* The number of gonorrhea infections in 15-19 year olds has continued to decline since the early 1980s, with chlamydia also declining over recent years.[1]
* Incidence (1/10,000) of chlamydia and gonorrhea infections among 15-19 year olds in 1994: 44.6 for chlamydia, and 1.2 for gonorrhea.[1]
* A total of nine cases of HIV transmissions have been notified to the national register among 15-19 year old boys and girls by 1992. In 1993-94 only one new HIV infection was reported.[1]
* Number of reported AIDS cases for the total population as of December 1993: 142.[7]

Homosexuality

* Legislation: In Finland the law prohibiting homosexual relations was repealed in 1971. Before that relations between women and relations between men were both illegal. Homosexuality was removed from the official classification of diseases in 1981.[8]
* The anti-discrimination legislation in the Finnish Penal Code and The Constitution was changed in 1995 to include discrimination based on sexual orientation.[9]
* A bill suggesting that two persons of the same sex could form a (legally binding) partnership was submitted to the Finnish Parliament on 28 May 1996, and is now in litigation.[10]
* Nearly 70% of the Finns polled show support for the same sex partnership law.[11]
* There is no discrimination of homosexuals in the military.[12]
* The promotion of same sex relationships is illegal under section 20:9.2 of the Penal Code which forbids public encouragement of fornication between members of the same sex.[13]

Prostitution[2]

* Prostitution is neither illegal nor regulated. Pimping and promoting prostitution are forbidden.

Pornography

* No information available.

Resources

Väestöliitto, Kalevankatu 16, 00100, Helsinki, Tel:(358 0) 616 221, Fax: (358 0) 6121 211.

References

1. Kosunen & M. Rimpela, "Improving Adolescent Sexual Health in Finland," <u>Choices</u>, (1996) Vol. 25 No 1, p. 18.

2. <u>The World Sex Guide</u>, "Prostitution in Finland," http://www.paranoia.com/faq/prostitution/Finland.html, Last update: 1996/04/30, (C) 1994,1995,1996, Atta and M. <u><an48932@anon.penet.fi></u>, received 6/17/96.

3. Lähteenmäki, S. Suhonen & K. Elnoma, "Use of Post-Coital Contraception in Finland is Increasing," <u>Planned Parenthood in Europe</u>,(1995) Vol. 24, No 2, August, p. 13.

4. Ritamies, "Finland Reduces Need For Abortion," <u>Planned Parenthood in Europe</u> (1993), Vol. 22 No 3, p. 13.

5. Rolston & A. Eggert, <u>Abortion in New Europe A Comparative Handbook</u> (Westport, CT, 1994) p. 88

6. National Abortion Campaign, <u>Abortion Laws in Europe (Amended Jan 1995)</u> (London, England: 1995).

7. United Nations, <u>Statistical Yearbook</u> (NY 1995), p. 96.

8. SETA, National Organization for Lesbian and Gay Men in Finland, <u>Queer Resources Directory</u>, "This is Finland 1/93, vol. 2," http://abacus.oxy.edu/qrd/world/europe/finland/this.is.finland-1,93, received 6/18/96.

9. Hiltunen, SETA, National Organization for Lesbian and Gay Men in Finland, <u>Queer Resources Directory</u>, http://abacus.oxy.edu/qrd/world/europe/finland/finnish.anti. discrimination, received 6/18/96.

10. Press Release By the MPs, 28 May 1996, <u>Queer Resources Directory</u>, "A Bill On the Partnership of Same Sex Couples,"http://abacus.oxy.edu/qrd/world/europe/ finland/mps.on.partnership.bill-05.28.96, received 6/18/96.

11. The Debate in the Parliament/Finland, <u>Queer Resources Directory</u>, "Congratulations to Island!," http://abacus.oxy.edu/qrd/world/europe/finland/ partnership.debate-06.05.96, received 6/18/96.

12. Alan F. Reekie, "Age of Consent Laws in the Council of Europe States in 1993," <http://ftp.tcp.com/qrd/world/europe/age.of.consent.laws-12.20.94>.

13. P. Snyder. <u>European Women's Almanac</u>. 1992. New York, NY: Columbia University Press, p. 99.

FRANCE
POPULATION: 58 MILLION

Capital:
Paris
(Population: 2 million/Metropolitan area: 9 million)

Major Cities & Population: Marseilles 800,550; Lyon 415,487; Toulouse 356,688; Nice 342,439; Strasbourg 252,338; Nantes 244,995

Ethnic Groups: 94% French

Languages: French(official), Breton spoke in Brittany, Basque & Catalan - Pyrenees region, Provencal spoken in Provere, Dutch is spoken in Flanders, German spoken in Alsace & Lorraine.

Major Religions: 76% Roman Catholicism; 5% Islam; 2% Protestantism; 1% Judaism; 16% Other

Annual Income Per Person: $20,600

Urban Population: 73%

Infant Mortality rate: 6 per 1,000 births

Life expectancy at birth: Females 82 years; Males 75 years

Literacy: 99%

Health Care System: National health care available.

References:
The World Almanac and Book of Facts 1996(1995) Mahwah, NJ: World Almanac Books
Microsoft Home; Encarta Encyclopedia, Microsoft Corporation (1996). (CD- ROM).

Sexual Activity

* Age of consent for heterosexual relations is 15 years of age.[1]
* Typical age of first intercourse: 16.5.[2]

Contraception

* France cut condom prices to encourage young people to use them.[3]
* In 1979, the French Parliament passed a bill that set strict limits on in vitro fertilization procedures and forestalled genetic engineers. The bill also bans lesbian couples and women past child-bearing age from artificial fertilization.[4]
* More than two-thirds of French women between the ages of 18 and 49 are now taking birth control pills.[5]
* For the first time, the French Roman Catholic bishops approved the use of condoms to help in the prevention of the HIV virus.[6]

Abortion

* Each year more than 2,000 French women go to England for an abortion, many of them because they have passed the 12-week limit.[7]
* 1/6th of all abortions are performed with RU-486; this pill can be taken by women under 35 and before the fifth week of pregnancy.[5]
* RU-486 was developed in France in the early 1980's and manufactured and marketed by Roussel Uclaf.[8]
* French Parliament passed a law that legalized abortion in 1979.[9]
* Abortion is legal until the 10th week of pregnancy. Parental consent is required for unmarried minors. The cost is covered by national health care.[10]

Sex Education[11]

* Sex education is a "preventive" approach.
* Sex education is usually linked to Biology, Health or Natural Sciences.
* The Family Planning Association is the main agency involved in sex education provisions. The sex education model consists of prevention, teacher training programs, as well as lectures to youth, thus addressing sex education as "Life Education."
* The FPA identified the public's attitudes towards sexuality on a scale from 1 (opposed) to 9 (well accepted); France was rated as a 5.

STD's, including AIDS

* There are 734 cases of AIDS reported to date.[12]
* WHO estimates that 90,000 adults are HIV positive.[13]

Homosexuality

* Age of consent for homosexuals is 15 years of age.[1]
* In 1985 France enacted regulations toward prohibiting discrimination against homosexuals.[14]
* France has provisions against discrimination of gays and lesbians at the workplace.[14]
* In autumn 1993, the French government adopted a law directing insurance companies to accept joint insurance coverage for non-married couples.[14]
* Proposals are currently being discussed to forbid lesbians from receiving artificial insemination.[14]

Prostitution[15]

* Prostitution is legal.
* Prostitutes are not allowed to tout on the public highway.
* Procuring is illegal as well. A prostitute is the only one person who can use the money she earns. If she is married and purchases food for the family her husband can be prosecuted as a procurer.

Pornography[16]

* The legal age for viewing pornography in France is age 18.

Resources

* Association Recherche Sexologique du Sud-Ouest (ARS SO); Bordeauz Rive Droite, Route Bergerac, F-33370, Fargues-St.-Hilaine.
* Fondateur de L'Association Mondiale de Sexology; 72, Quai Louis Bleriot, 75016, Paris.
* Sexologies-European Journal of Medical Sociology; 21, Place Alexandre Labadie, 13001 Marseilles.
* Syndicat National des Medecins Sexologues(SNMS); 77 Rue Lakana, IF-37000, Tours, France.
* Mouvement Francais pour le Planning Familial (MFPF), 4 Square St Irenee, 75011 Paris.

References

1. Alan F. Reekie, "Age of Consent Laws in the Council of Europe States in 1993," <http://ftp.tcp.com/qrd/world/europe/age.of.consent.laws-12.20.94>.
2. ACSsF Investigators, "AIDS and Sexual Behavior in France," Nature (Dec. 3, 1992) vol. 360(4603), p. 397-407.
3. "France Cuts Condom Prices." New York Times (Dec. 5, 1993), vol. 143, sec.1, p. 14.
4. "France Restricts Fertilization Procedures." Contemporary Sexuality (August, 1994), vol. 28(8), p. 14.
5. SOCIETE, "20 years of Abortion," News from France (February 3, 1996) vol.95.02, http://www.info-france.org/newstatmnt/nff2/societe1.html (retrieved 6/20/96)
6. Facts of File, Weekly World News Digest (February 12, 1996).
7. Henshaw, "Abortion Services Under National Health Insurance: The Examples of England and France," Viewpoint (March/April 1996), vol. 26(2), p. 87.
8. C. Ellerston et al. "Expanding Access To Emergency Contraception in Developing Countries." Studies in Family Planning (Sept./Oct. 1995.) Vol. 26 n.(5) p. 251-263.
9. B. Rolston & A. Eggert, Abortion in the New Europe: A Comparative Handbook. (Westport, CT: Greenwood, 1994.)
10 G. Kelly, Sexuality Today (Guilford, CT: Brown & Benchmark, 1996) p. 327.
11. D. Vilar, "School Sex Education: Still a Priority in Europe." Planned Parenthood in Europe (1994) vol. 23(3), p. 8-12.
12. "HIV.NET" http://www.hiv.net (retrieved 6/18/96)
13. World Health Organization, Global Programme on AIDS. p. 1-4 http://gpawww. who.ch/aidscase/dec/1995/hivtext.html (retrieved 6/24/96)
14. A. Duda Comparative Survey of the Legal and Societal Situation of Homosexuals in Europe (updated version) http://www. casti.com/FQRD/assocs/ilga/euroletter/ 35-survey.html (retrieved 6/20/96).
15. Prostitution in France. http://www.paranoia.com/faq/prostitution/France.html. (retrieved 6/14/96)
16. Restricted Access. http://www.pinkboard.com.au:80/r.html (retrieved 6/19/96).

GERMANY
(FEDERAL REPUBLIC OF GERMANY)
POPULATION: 81 MILLION

Capital:
Berlin
(population: 3.3 million)

Major Cities & Populations: Berlin 3,301,000; Hamburg 1,594,000; Munich 1,189,000; Cologne 928,000

Ethnic Groups: German 92%; Turkish 2%; Italian 1%; Yugoslavian 1%; Greek 0.4%

Languages: German (official)

Major Religions: Protestant 45%; Roman Catholic 37%; other 18%

Annual Income per Person: $17,000

Urban Population: 85%

Infant Mortality: 8 per 1,000 live births

Life Expectancy: male 72; female 78

Adult Literacy: 99%

Health Care System: Socialized system

References:
CIA 1995 Fact Book, (retrieved July 6, 1996) http://www.odci.gov/cia/publications/95fact/nz.html
Masur, Joshua M.K., Women of the World - Germany: Overview, Center for Reproductive Law & Policy, http://www.echonyc.com/~jmkm/wotw/germany.overview.html, (last updated August 27, 1995, retrieved June 23, 1996).
Rayner, Caroline, Encyclopedic World Atlas, Oxford Univ. Press, New York: 1994.

Sexual   Activity

* The legal age for consent is 14.[1]
* The birth rate in eastern regions of Germany has dropped by more than 30% since reunification.[2]

Contraception

* Oral contraceptive pills, IUDs, barrier methods and sterilization are available and covered by insurance.[3]
* Women under 20 years of age in Germany's eastern states can legally obtain oral contraception free.[2]
* 50% of women in Germany's western states and 61% of the women in Germany's eastern states use oral contraceptives. The next most popular contraceptive methods are some sort of barrier (10%) or IUD (13%). Sterilization is the method of choice for nearly 7% of western states' women and for 3% of eastern states' women, while 7% of western states' women and nearly 9% of eastern states' women choose natural methods of contraception.[4]
* Tetragynon®, a version of the Yuzpe regimen, is sold as a post-coital pregnancy prevention and is purported to reduce the chances of pregnancy by 75%.[3]
* Oral and emergency contraception methods are available only by prescription. However, some health facilities provide 24-hr telephone referrals to sources of emergency contraception.[5]
* Due to the AIDS crisis, the use of condoms doubled in the late 80's, but young people are shy about purchasing and using them.[6]
* The uncertainty of social situations and the risk that pregnancy may reduce women's employability has prompted more women in the eastern states to seek sterilization. Some employers are advising women looking for work to be sterilized.[2]

Abortion

* Current abortion law is based upon a 1993 Federal Constitutional Court decision and the Penal Code. In May of 1993, the Court ruled that abortion is not punishable if it is performed within the first trimester at the woman's request and with evidence that the woman has obtained counseling within 3 days prior to the abortion. The Penal Code allows abortion with the woman's consent if the woman's life is endangered or

if the fetus "suffers from such irremedial damage" that continuation of the pregnancy could not be demanded of the woman.[7]

* In January of 1996, the German Parliament promulgated that abortion is legal within the first trimester with counseling by a physician and outside counseling center, with the priority being to protect the unborn child while allowing the woman to choose. The Parliament also legalized abortion in cases of rape, incest, and life and health endangerment of the woman.[7]

* The German Parliament has reduced punishments for performing or seeking illegal abortions, while ruling that fathers must provide financial support to their pregnant partners. Parents face up to two years in prison if they try to persuade their pregnant daughters to have abortions.[8]

* The Court interprets Article 1 of the Basic Law to protect human life of the unborn. ("The dignity of man is inviolable. To respect and protect it shall be the duty of all public authority."[7]

* Legal abortions may be obtained by women over 18 years of age without parental consent. Physicians can allow abortions for 14 year olds if the girl fully understands the ramifications of the abortion.[9]

* Legal abortions are covered by statutory health insurance plans.[7]

* Abortion is still considered shameful. Anti-abortion sentiment is precipitating demonstrations and picketing outside abortion clinics in Germany.[9]

* In 1994, the abortion rate was 0.9 per 1,000 in the West, and 3.2 per 1,000 in the East.[7]

Sex Education

* The Pregnancy and Family Support Act of 1992 makes it the duty of the Federal and Laender governments to improve sex education.[3]

* Pro Familia, Germany's family planning association, provides counseling and sex education. There is some public funding for sex education, but only a fraction of what was initially planned.[10]

* Information and focus in AIDS education will be to provide counseling and care for HIV/AIDS patients and the prevention of discrimination towards persons with positive HIV/AIDS status. The mass media provides messages promoting safe sex, and the schools encourage AIDS education.[11]

STDs, including AIDS

* The major means of HIV transmission in Germany is homosexual or bisexual relations.[12]
* There were approximately 43,00 total AIDS cases reported in Germany as of December, 1995.[13]
* Women comprised 9.7% of the AIDS cases in 1992.[3]
* The Federal Venereal Disease Control Act (FVDC) of 1953 focuses on syphilis, gonorrhea, chancroid and lymphogranulomatosis and includes strict regulations with reporting and notification requirements. While the disease is transmissible, people with STDs are prohibited from breast-feeding, having sexual intercourse, and performing professional activities which carry the risk of transmitting the disease.[11]
* The 1961 Federal Epidemics Control Act (FECA) makes communicable diseases the responsibility of the Public Health Service and includes the surveillance of infected persons.[11]
* There are no AIDS laws per se. FVDC and FECA are not seen as pertinent to AIDS. However, according to a judgment by the 1988 Supreme Court, if an HIV+ person transmits the virus through sexual intercourse, a penalty of up to five years in prison may be adjudged.[11]
* The opening of the wall between the East and West and the rise of unrestricted travel raises the chances that STDs will be harder to contain or trace.[6]

Homosexuality

* A minimum of 10,000 homosexual men were forced by the Nazis to wear pink triangles and be confined to concentration campus during World War II.[14]
* By 1948, some toleration of homosexuality had begun, but it took until 1968-69 for the Imperial Penal Code of 1871, Paragraph 175 and criminalization of homosexuality (1897) to be abolished.[14]
* In June, 1992, the German State Brandenburg enacted a new constitution instituting State recognition of non-marriage partnerships.[15]
* In 1993, Berlin included sexual identity as a non-discrimination criteria in its constitution. Also in 1993, the German State Thuringia included sexual orientation as a non-discrimination criteria in its constitution pending approval by a referendum in 1994.[15]
* Judges have interpreted the right to marriage as heterosexual, but family law does not specify gender. Same sex couples appealed the court decision. The Court has denied the appeal, but emphasized the need for legal protection for same sex partnerships.[15]

* Gays cannot be excluded from military service, but homosexual relations between military personnel on duty is illegal.[16]
* Age of consent for homosexual and lesbian relations is 14.[17]

Prostitution[18]

* Prostitution is legal in Germany, but does not carry the status of an ordinary profession. Communities can limit areas used and the times of day prostitutes work. Prostitutes must be registered with the health authorities.
* Pimping and promoting prostitution are illegal.
* Street prostitutes, sex shops and clubs are most often found near railway stations.
* Sex shops sell magazines with information for finding prostitutes.
* EROS Centers can be found where prostitutes rent a room and sit in the window to lure customers.
* A new law allows the prosecution of Germans having sex with children in other countries who have not reached the age of consent.

Pornography[18]

* Child pornography is considered to be depictions of sexual acts involving children under 14.
* S/M, zoophily and toilet sex are legal. However, making of S/M and zoophily material is illegal.
* An October, 1994 law makes possession of child pornography illegal; possession of S/M or zoophily is legal.

Resources

Pro Familia: Deutsche, Gesellschaft fur Familienplanung, Sexualpadagogik, und Sexualberatung, Stresemann Allee 3, 60596 Frankfurt am Main, Germany

National AIDS Committee (Nationaler AIDS-Beirat - NAB), Federal Ministry for Health, 53108 Bonn, Germany; Tel: (228) 941-3200

German Society for Sexual Research (Deutsche Gesellschaft fur Sexualforschung - DGSF), c/o Klinik fuer Psychotherapie und Psychosomatik, Niemannsweg 147, 24105 Kiel, Germany; Tel: (431) 597-2655

References

1. J. Masur, Women of the World - Germany: Overview, Center for Reproductive Law & Policy. http://www.echonys.com/~jmkm/wotw/germany.overview.html, last updated August 27, 1995, retrieved June 23, 1996.
2. Alan F. Reekie, "Age of Consent Laws in the Council of Europe States in 1993," <http://ftp.tcp.com/qrd/world/europe/age.of.consent.laws-12.20.94>.
3. L. Aresin, "East Germany Two Years After Unification," Planned Parenthood in Europe, 1993, Vol. 22 (1), p. 11-12.
4. J. Masur, Women of the World - Germany: Family Planning, Center for Reproductive Law & Policy. http://www.echonys.com/~jmkm/wotw/germany.overview.html, last updated August 27, 1995, retrieved June 23, 1996.
5. C. Ellertson et al, "Expanding Access to Emergency Contraception in Developing Countries," Studies in Family Planning, 1995, Vol. 26 (5).
6. H. Neumann et al, "Enlightment Prevents Fear of AIDS,", Planned Parenthood in Europe, 1990,Vol 19, (1), p. 14
7 J. Masur, Women of the World - Germany: Abortion, Center for Reproductive Law & Policy. http://www.echonys.com/~jmkm/wotw/germany.overview.html, last updated August 27, 1995, retrieved June 23, 1996.
8. Abortion Update, Contempory Sexuality, July 1994, Vol. 28 (7), p. 7.
9. J. Von Baross, "German Constitutional Court Rejects Abortion Compromise," Planned Parenthood in Europe, 1993, Vol. 22 (3), p. 14-16.
10. J. Von Baross, "The 'Yo-yo Effect' of Public Family Planning Funding in Germany," Planned Parenthood in Europe, 1994, Vol 23 (1), p. 5-7.
11. J. Masur, Women of the World - Germany: STDs and HIV/AIDS, Center for Reproductive Law & Policy. http://www.echonys.com/~jmkm/wotw/germany.overview.html, last updated August 27, 1995, retrieved June 23, 1996.
12. E. Jamison, et al, World Population Profile: 1994, U.S. Department of Commerce Economics and Statistical Administraion Bureau of Census, Washington, D.C.
13. Provisional Working Estimates of Adult HIV Prevalence as of end of 1995 by Country, WHO. <http://gpa.who.ch/aidscase/dec1995/hivtext.html> (retrieved June 24, 1996.)
14. W. Dynes, Encyclopedia of Homsexuality Vol. 1, New York: Guiford, 1990.
15. C. Duda, "Comparative Survey of the Legal and Societal Situation of Homosexuality in Europe, <http://www.casti.com/FQRD/assocs.ilga/euroletter/35-survey.html. (last updated August, 1995, retrieved June 28, 1996).
16. A. Riding, "In NATO, Only US and British Ban Gay Soldiers," New York Times, November 13, 1992, p. A12.
17. Alan F. Reekie, "Age of Consent Laws in the Council of Europe States in 1993," <http://ftp.tcp.com/qrd/world/europe/age.of.consent.laws-12.20.94>.
18. The World Sex Guide. <an48932@anon.penet.fi> http://www.paranoia.com/faq/prostitution/Germany.html, last updated April 30, 1996. (retrieved June 21, 1996).

GREECE
POPULATION: 10.5 MILLION

Capital:
A t h e n s
(population: 3 million)

Major cities & Populations: Thessoloniki: 378,000

Ethnic Groups: Greek 96%; Macedonian 2%; Turkish 1%; Albanian & Slav

Languages: Greek (official), English & French

Major Religions: Greek Orthodox 98% (official); Muslim 2%

Annual Income Per Person: $6,230

Urban Population: 63%

Infant Mortality: 8 per 1,000 births

Life Expectancy: Females 81 years; Males 75 years

Adult Literacy: 93%

Health Care System: Physicians: 1 per 303 persons; Hospital beds: 1 per 199 persons

---

References:
Encyclopedic World Atlas (1994) NY: Oxford University Press.
The World Almanac and Book of Facts 1996 (1995) Mahwah, NJ: World Almanac Books

Sexual Activity

* Age of consent for heterosexual relations is 15 years of age.[1]
* Teen pregnancies are rising. In 1985 they accounted for 5.4% of all pregnancies but this had doubled by to over 10% by 1989.[2]

Contraception

* Until 1980, family planning was illegal in Greece; abortion was mainly used as a form of birth control, and despite being illegal, it was widespread.[3]
* The condom represents the main form of modern contraception (35% of all users).[4]
* Over 60% of women rely on withdrawal as their only contraceptive method. [5]
* The pill has been available without a prescription since 1963.[5]
* The cost of modern contraception is not expensive in comparison with the cost of abortion: The Pill: 900-1,200 drachmas (US $35-45) per month; The IUD cost 3,000 drachmas (US $115) with free insertion through the family planning centers; The condom: 80-100 drachmas (US $3-$4) per condom.[4]

Abortion

* Abortion is the primary method of family planning, despite the increasing availability of most modern forms of contraception.[4]
* Until the Second World War, abortion was strictly opposed except on medical grounds. Abortion laws were liberalized in 1978, and again in 1986, allowing a women to have a free abortion in a public hospital up to the 12th week (later abortions are permitted on various grounds).[3]
* Women under 18 must have parental consent.[2]
* Roughly two out of three women have had an abortion with a resulting ratio of 1.3 live births to 1.8 abortions per woman.[5]
* Private abortions cost about US $200 and are usually performed immediately, in contrast to the state system which requires bureaucratic procedures and consequent delays.[5]

Sex Education

* Sex education does not exist in the school curricula; in fact Greece is one of the few European countries without sex education.[6]
* Although family planning clinics were first established in the early 1980s, they are not currently involved in school sex education per se; they are involved in trying to influence public and policial opinion and the training of health workers. [7]

STDs, including AIDS

* Greece has one of the lowest rates of AIDS in Europe.[8]
* In 1993 the Center for AIDS Research in Greece estimated that 10,000 to 15,000 people in the country were infected with HIV.[8]
* There are 1,217 cases of AIDS.[9]

Homosexuality

* In 1987 a common age of consent of 15 was introduced; before then the age of consent was higher for gay men (17 compared to 16).[2]
* A law introduced in 1981 on public health allows forced testing of gay men for STD's. It has been used by police to harass gays.[2]
* Greece has policies excluding persons who engage in homosexual behavior from military service.[10]

Prostitution

* Heterosexual prostitution is legal in Greece, while homosexual prostitution is banned.[11]
* The Greek government recently unveiled a plan to make prostitutes retire at 55 with the state providing social and medical benefits.[12]
* Registered prostitutes are required to attend clinics periodically for testing and treatment.[12]

Pornography

* Both heterosexual and homosexual pornography is a thriving industry.[13]
* Bookstores and X-rated back rooms of video stores display heterosexual and homosexual materials on adjacent shelves.[13]
* Many Greek paintings (erotic art) show sexual intercourse, fellatio, orgies, pedophilic behavior and a variety of other sexual behaviors.[14]

Resources

*Family Planning Association of Greece, 121 Solonos Street, Athens 106 78
*Greek Society of Andrology and Sexology, Chalcocondili 50, Athens.

References

1. Alan F. Reekie, "Age of Consent Laws in the Council of Europe States in 1993," <http://ftp.tcp.com/qrd/world/europe/age.of.consent.laws-12.20.94>.

2. P. Snyder, <u>The European Women's Almanac</u> (NY: Columbia Univ. Press, 1992), p. 152.

3. United Nations, <u>Abortion Policies: A Global Review</u> (NY, 1992), p. 31-33.

4. P. Tseperi & E. Mestheneos, "Paradoxes in the Costs of Family Planning in Greece," <u>Planned Parenthood in Europe</u> (1994), 23(1), p. 14.

5. D. Naziri, "The Trivality of Abortion in Greece," <u>Planned Parenthood in Europe</u> (1991), 20(2), p. 12.

6. D. Vilar, "Schhol Sex Education: Still a Priority in Europe," <u>Planned Parenthood in Europe</u> (1994), 23(3), p. 8-12.

7. L. Mestheneos, PPA Profile: Greece," <u>Planned Parenthood in Europe</u> (1992), 21(1), p. 36-37.

8. G. Curtis, <u>Greece: A Country Study</u> (1994) Federal Research Division, Library of Congress, p. 137.

9. HIV.NET "Epidemiology: Transmission Cases" http://www.hiv.net (retrieved 6/26/96)

10. S. Harris, "Military Policies Regarding Homosexual Behavior: An International Survey," <u>Journal of Homosexuality</u> (1991), 21(4), p. 67-74.

11. A. Duda, "Comparative Survey of the Legal and Societal Situation of Homosexuals in Europe," http://www.casti.com/FQRD/assocs/ilga/euroletter/35-survey.html (retrieved June 26, 1996).

12. <u>The World Sex Guide: Greece</u>. Last update 1996/04/30. (C) 1994, 1995, 1996 Atta and M. <an48932@anon.penet.fi> http://www.paranoia.com/faq/prostitution (retrieved June 26, 1996).

13. A. Richlin, <u>Pornography and Representation in Greece and Rome</u> (NY: Oxford University Press (1994), p. 54.

14. G. Kelly. <u>Sexuality Today</u> (Guilford, CT: Brown & Benchmark, 1995) p. 430.

HUNGARY
POPULATION: 10.3 MILLION

Capital:
Budapest
(population: 2 million)

Major Cities and Populations Debrecen 217,000; Miskolc 191,000

Ethnic Groups: Hungarian 90%, Gypsy 4%, German 2,5%

Languages: Hungarian (Magyar)

Major Religions: Roman Catholic 67%, Calvanist 20%, Lutheran 5%

Income Per Capita: $5,500

Urban Population: 63%

Infant Mortality: 12 per 1000 live births

Life Expectancy: Female 76 years, male 68 years

Adult Literacy: 99%

Health Care System: The Ministry of Health administers the state health service. Since 1974, 99% of the population was covered and was eligible for free health care. Limited private practice is permitted.

References:
Worldmark Encyclopedia of the Nations: Europe, Vol. 5, Eighth Edition, pp. 195-206, Gale Research Inc, Detroit, 1995.
The World Almanac and Book of Facts 1996 (1995), Mahwah, NJ: World Almanac Books

Sexual   Activity[1]

* The age of consent for sexual activity for heterosexuals is 14.

Contraception[2]

* Postinor, a form of emergency contraception, was developed in Hungary.
* Postinor was originally promoted as the ideal method of contraception for people with infrequent sexual contacts, and it soon became one of the most widely used forms of birth control.
* It is believed that most Hungarian women do not keep a supply of Postinor on hand for emergencies, but that younger women are more likely to carry it in their purses.
* Though there is little national data about such statistics, users of emergency contraception tend to be young, unmarried women, who switch to oral contraception when in a stable relationship, and then to IUDs when their families are completed.

Abortion

* A new "law on the protection of fetal life" was passed in December of 1992.[3]
* Abortion is available up to 12 weeks, with exceptions made for the following reasons: health risk to mother or fetus, rape or other sexual crime, or due to the crisis situation of the pregnant woman.
* Minors must have parental consent.[3]
* Counselling is mandatory. Women must wait three days after counselling but must have the abortion within eight days of the counselling.[3]
* The "crisis situation" is defined by the woman herself, but is not discussed, as it is considered a private matter.[3]
* Since the new law, abortion rates have declined.[5]
* Public opinion holds that it is the right of each woman to decide whether to terminate a pregnancy or to give birth. It is also public opinion that the father/spouse/partner should also be given consideration about such decisions.[3]
* Though most Hungarians believe that life begins in the womb, this belief does not affect abortion arguments for socio-economic or health reasons.[4]

Sex Education[5]

* Some sex education subjects exist in school curricula, though it is linked with Biology, Health, or the Natural Sciences.
* There is sex education for pre-adolescents, focusing on biological facts of reproduction and puberty.
* There is no opportunity for formal sex education training for teachers.
* Family Planning Association is the main agency involved in sex education.

STDs, including AIDS

* HIV testing is mandatory for STD patients.[6]
* Hungary has reported 190 AIDS cases since 1986.[7]
* Primary transmission of HIV appears to be through homosexual contact.[7]
* People are infected at the rate of 19 per million.[7]

Homosexuality

* Age of consent for homosexuals (men and women) is 18.[1]
* Section 199 of the Penal Code refers to homosexuality as "illicit sexual practicies."[8]
* In March of 1995, Hungary became the first Eastern European country to extend traditional common-law marriage rights to homosexual couples. However, formal, civil marriages are not legal for homosexuals.[9]

Prostitution[10]

* Prostitution has been legal since 1992.
* Prostitutes may be found in clubs (La Dolce Vita), bars, hotels, and through the newspaper "Expressz" under the headline "Szexpartnert," where you may find agencies and massage parlors.

Pornography[11]

* The legal age for viewing pornography is 18.

Resources

Pro Familia Hungarian Scientific Society, Buai Laszl u. 2. III. em. 1, 1024 Budapest, Hungary.

References

1. Alan F. Reekie, "Age of Consent Laws in the Council of Europe States in 1993," <http://ftp.tcp.com/qrd/world/europe/age.of.consent.laws-12.20.94>.

2. Sharon Camp, "Postinor-the Unique Method of Emergency Contraception Developed in Hungary," Planned Parenthood in Europe, Vol. 24, No. 2, August, pp. 23-24, 1995.

3. Abortion Laws in Europe (amended Jan 1995).

4. Marietta Pongracz, "Induced Abortion in Hungary Today: Results of a Public Opinion Poll," Planned Parenthood in Europe, Vol. 20, No. 2, p. 8, 1991.

5. Duarte Vilar, "School Sex Education: Still a Priority in Europe," Duarte Vilar, "School Sex Education: Still a Priority in Europe," Planned Parenthood in Europe, Vol. 23, No. #, pp. 8-12, (1994).

6. AIDS 1993, March, pp. 393-400.

7. HIV.NET, <http://hiv.net/hiv.us/epidem/epidem.htm>, 8/27/96.

8. P. Snyder. The European Women's Almanac. 1992, New York, NY: Columbia University Press. p. 166.

9. Blaise Szolgyemy, <http://www.qrd.org/qrd/world/> 3/9/95.

10. The World Sex Guide, "Prostitution in: Hungary," <http://www.paranoia.com/faq/prostitution/Hungary.html> last updated 4/30/96.

11. Restricted Access, <http://www.pinkboard.com.au:80/r.html>, 8/27/96.

INDIA
POPULATION: 936.5 MILLION

Capital:
New Delhi
(population: 5.7 million)

Major Cities & Populations: Calcutta 9 million; Bombay 8 million; Delhi 5.7 million; Madras 4 million;

Ethnic Groups: Indo-Aryan 72%, Dravidian 25%

Languages: Hindi (official), English and over 24 different languages

Major Religions: Hindu 80%, Muslim 14%, Christian 2.4%, Sikh 2%, Buddhist 0.7%

Annual Income Per Person: $330

Urban Population: 28%

Infant Mortality: 76 per 1,000 births

Life Expectancy: Females 60 years; Males 58 years

Adult Literacy: 43%

Health Care System: Gov't responsible for all health care; hospitals; public/private physicians

References:
"India" The CIA World Fact Book 1995
Encyclopedic World Atlas (1994) NY: Oxford University Press
Roemer, Milton I. (1993) National Health Systems of the World; The Issues. Vol II, Oxford University Press.
The World Almanac and Book of Facts 1996 (1995) Mahwah, NJ World Almanac Books

Sexual Activity[1]

* All types of sexual interaction before marriage is forbidden; total self-restraint is advocated. Even the discussion of sex is taboo but this is slowly weakening. A study revealed that almost 16% of rural boys and 9% of college males had a sexual experience. More than 80% of the boys had their first sexual contact with a prostitute and 80% had never used a condom. 16% reported that their first sexual contact had been with a girl friend of almost the same age group.
* The mean age at first coitus: 18 years.

Contraception

* The government of India's plan to "control the population" is to decrease the present level of approximately 33 births per 1,000 population to the low 20,s by the year 2000.[2]
* At present, the Indian government favors sterilization, which many reject because it is irreversible.[3]
* In 1989, 43% of Indians used contraception. 72% of all contraceptive users relied heavily on sterilization. In 1993, 43% of all sterilizations were performed on women. 11.8% used condoms. 4.2% used IUD's. 3.1% used pills.[4] The government which for many years has offered cash incentives to both acceptors and providers of male and female sterilization, has in the past few years increased it's promotion of the pill, condoms and IUD's which are now offered free of charge.[2]
* A group of Indian scientists is studying a contraceptive injection for men that they believe will become more popular than the vasectomy because it will be easily reversible.[5]
* Emergency contraception: not yet available.[6]

Abortion

* Unless a medical emergency exists, a legal abortion must be performed during the first 20 weeks of gestation by a registered physician in a government hospital.[7]
* A legal abortion is free of charge only if it is performed in a government hospital. These hospitals are often inaccessible, therefore the number of illegal and/or unregistered abortions are estimated to be between 2 million and 6 million annually.[7]
* In 1991-1992 alone, of the approximately 6.7 million induced abortions, only 600,000 were legally performed.[8]

* It is estimated that unsafe abortions account for 20% of maternal deaths in India.[7]
* Female feticide is common although there are no adequate statistics available on the subject.[6]
* In an effort to halt widespread abortions of female fetuses, the Indian Parliament passed a law prohibiting doctors from telling expectant parents of their offspring's gender. The bill also bans the advertisement and performance of ultrasounds solely to determine gender.[9]
* RU 486 (non-surgical "abortion pill"): not yet available in India.[6]

Sex   Education

* There has been no sex education at any level in the past.[6]
* Sex education is not taught in schools because society believes it would "spoil the minds" of the children.[1]
* The Ministry of Health and Family Welfare recently began coordinating primary and adult education programs and is promoting its family planning agenda in rural areas.[9]

STD's, including AIDS

* It is estimated that approximately 90 million adults are affected by STD's.[9]
* There are approximately 372 STD clinics located across the country.[9]
* It is estimated that India will surpass Africa as the "epi-center of AIDS" in 5 years and is likely to have more HIV-positive residents than the rest of the world combined.[10]
* 1.5 million people in India are estimated to be currently infected with HIV/AIDS. As of Sept 1994, the government reported that 15,692 individuals tested HIV-positive.[9]
* Concerned about the spread of AIDS, Indian health officials have begun campaigning for the free distribution of condoms in prison.[10]
* India has no laws barring prostitutes from continuing their trades even after they discover that they are HIV-positive.[11]

Homosexuality[12]

* According to a survey done between 1982 & 1984 by the United States Department of Defense, India reported to have policies excluding persons who engage in homosexual behavior from military service

* 32% of Indians reported that some form of homosexual behavior is a punishable offense
* 9% of Indians reported that the government minimizes the existence of homosexual behavior in the military.

Prostitution

* Prostitution is technically illegal but widely tolerated.[13]
* According to health authorities, Bombay has over 100,000 prostitutes.[14]
* 20% of the prostitutes in Bombay are under the age of 18, about half are infected with HIV.[15]
* In south-western India, thousands of people have been dedicating their daughters to a religiously sanctioned life of prostitution for well over a millennium.[16] These girls, some as young as 6, are initiated into a life of sexual slavery as servants of the gods.[17]
* Childrens advocacy groups estimate that 300,000-400,000 children in India are involved in the sex industry.[18]
* Legal age of consent for sex: 16.[13]

Pornography

* Data not available on the subject.

Resources

Sex Education, Counseling, Research Training Centre (SECRT) Family Planning Association of India (FPAI), Fifth Floor, Cecil Court, Mahakavi Bhushan Marg, Bombay 400 039. Phone: 91-22/287-4689.

Indian Association of Sex Educators, Counselors, and Therapists (IASECT), 203 Sukhsagar, N. S. Patkar Marg., Bombay 400 007. Phone: 91-22/361-2027.

Parivar Seva Sanstha 28, Defence Colony Market, New Delhi 110-024. Phone: 91-11/461-7712.

References

1. V. Sharma & A. Sharma. "The letter-box approach: A model for sex education in an orthodox society" Journal of Family Welfare (Dec. 1995) Vol. 41, No. 4., p. 31.
2. J. Stevens & C. Stevens. "Introductory small cash incentives to promote child spacing in India" Studies in Family Planning (May/June 1992) Vol. 23, No. 3., p. 171.
3. "Issues in Focus: India", Audobon (July/Aug 1994) p. 58.
4. J. M. K. Masur. "Center for reproductive law and policy" http://www.echonyc.com/~jmkm/wotw/only. Last updated 27 Aug 1995.
5. "Studies in Short: Indian researchers test reversible male sterilization" Contemporary Sexuality (Aug 95) Vol. 29, No. 8, p. 4.
6. S. Chandrasekhar. India's Abortion Experience 1972-1992 (University of Washington Press, 1994) p. 130.
7. United Nations, Abortion Policies: A Global Review (New York, 1992) p. 57.
8. J. M. K. Masur. "Center for reproductive law and policy" http://www.echonyc.com/~jmkm/wotw/only. Last updated 27 Aug 1995.
9. "Sexuality and the Law: Indian Parliament bans mention of fetus's gender" Contemporary Sexuality (Sep 94) Vol. 28, No. 9, p. 13,15.
10. "International Update: India will be new AIDS epicenter" Contemporary Sexuality (April 1995) Vol. 29, No. 4, p. 5.
11. J. W. Anderson. "AIDS nears epidemic rate in India: prostitution, blood supply, drug use blamed for spread of disease" The Washington Post (Sept 14 1992) Vol. 115, p. A1, col. 3.
12. S. Harris. "Military Policies Regarding Homosexual Behavior: An International Survey" Journal of Homosexuality (1991) Vol. 21, (4), p. 67-74.
13. "Prostitution in India" The World Sex Guide, /www.paranoia.com/faq/prostitution/India.html Last update: 1996/04/30.
14. J. W. Anderson. "AIDS nears epidemic rate in India: prostitution, blood supply, drug use blamed for spread of disease" The Washington Post (Sept 14 1992) Vol. 115, p. A1, col. 3.
15. "International Update: Nepali girls enslaved in Bombay brothels" Contemporary Sexuality (Sept 95) Vol. 29, No. 9, P. 9.
16. A. Sachs. "The Last Commodity: Child Prostitution in the Developing World" World Watch (July/Aug 1994) p. 25-30.
17. C. Aziz. "A Life of Hell for the wife of a god. (religious cults forcing young Indian girls into sexual slavery)" The Guardian (June 10 1995) p. 25(1).
18. J. Kennedy. "Opinion/Essays: Crime Bill Cracks Down on Child Exploitation" The Christian Science Monitor (Sept 6 1994) Vol. 86, No. 198, p. 19.

IRAN
POPULATION: 65 MILLION

Capital:
T e h r a n
(population: 6 million)

Major Cities & Poplations: Tehran: 6,043,000

Ethnic   Groups: Persian 46%;   Azerbaijani 17%;
Kurdish 9%; Gilaki 5%; plus Luri,
Mazandaran, Baluchi, & Arab

Languages: Farsi (Persian) 46%,   Kurdish,
Baluchi, Turkic, Arabic & French

Major   Religions: Shiite Muslim 91%; Sunni Muslim 8%

Annual Income Per Person: $2,320

Urban   Population: 57%

Infant   Mortality: 55 per 1,000 births

Life Expectancy: Female 68 years;   Males 67 years

Adult   Literacy: 51%

Health Care System: Physicians: 1 per 2,000 persons

References:
Encyclopedic World Atlas (1994) NY: Oxford University Press
The World Almanac and Book of Facts 1996 (1995) Mahwah, NJ: World Almanac Books

Sexual Activity

* Polygyny is regulated by Islamic custom, which permits a man to have as many as four wives simultaneously, provided that he treats them equally.[1]
* On May 16th 1993 the Iranian Parliament ratified a bill aimed at encouraging couples to have no more than three children. Legislation will grant special government benefits to the first three children only. This rule took affect in 1994.[2]

Contraception

* The goal of the Social and Cultural Development Plan is to reduce the total fertility rate to four children per woman by the year 2011.[3]
* The Government has proposed to raise levels of contraception use to 24% of women of childbearing age and to prevent 1 million unwanted births.[3]
* The Health Ministry distributes condoms, IUDs and birth control pills for free. Vasectomies are also free.[4]

Abortion[3]

* In 1973, induced abortion was legalized in Iran.
* After the revolution in 1979, abortion was once again made illegal on most grounds. Abortion is currently prohibited on all grounds except to save the life of a pregnant woman.

Sex Education[4]

* In order to get a marriage license, couples must take segregated course in family planning.

STDs, including AIDS[5]

* In 1993 there was 92 cases of AIDS in Iran.

Homosexuality[6]

* Homosexuality is illegal in Iran.
* Under Islamic law in Iran gays and lesbians can be executed.

Prostitution[7]

* Prostitution is illegal in Iran.
* On May 6, 1994 an American woman, Mary Jones of Texas was arrested and convicted for prostitution in Iran. She recieved 80 lashes as her punishment.

Pornography[8]

* Pornography is illegal in Iran.
* The Iranian Parliament has approved legislation providing for capital punishment for producers & distributors of pornographic videotapes.
* The bill which provides a maximum five years prison term and $100,000 in fines for first offenders, said the principal promoters of pornographic videos can receive the death penalty.

Resources

*Islamic Women's Institute (13643), No. 1-275 Hedayat St., N. Saddi, Tehran, Iran
PH: 21 3115656; FAX: 21 3116201.

References

1. H.C. Metz, <u>Iran: A Country Study</u> (1987) Federal Research Division, Library of Congress, p. 111.

2. T. Carrington. "Iran Enacts Family Size Rule" <u>The Wall Street Journal</u>, May 17 (1993) p.A13

3. United Nations, <u>Abortion Policies: A Global Review</u> (NY, 1992), p.63-64.

4. Internationa Update, <u>Contemporary sexuality</u>, October 1996, p. 9.

5. United Nations, <u>Statistical Yearbook</u> (New York, 1995), p. 95.

6. B. Boxall, "Three Foreign Gays Seek US Asylum."<u>LA Times</u> (April 30, 1993), p. B3.

7. R. Sepehrrad, "Eighty Lashes In Iran," The Washington Post (May 25, 1994), p. A22.

8. "Iranian Approves Death Penalty for Makers Of Video Pornography," <u>New York Times</u> (December 21, 1993), p. A5.

IRELAND
POPULATION: 3.5 MILLION

Capital:
Dublin
(population: 478,000)

Major Cities & Populations:	Cork 127,000
Ethnic Groups:	Celtic, English minority
Languages:	English predominates, Irish (Gaelic) spoken by minority
Major Religions:	Roman Catholic 93%; Anglican 3%
Annual Income per Person:	$13,100
Urban Population:	57%
Infant Mortality:	7 per 1,000 births
Life Expectancy:	Females 79 years; Males 73 years
Adult Literacy:	100%
Health Care System:	Physicians: 1 per 681 persons

References:
Encyclopedic World Atlas (1994) NY: Oxford University Press.
The World Almanac and Book of Facts 1996 (1995) Mahwah, NJ: World Almanac Books.

Sexual Activity

* The age of consent is 18.[1]
* Of 195 women obtaining abortions in England, 1.5% had their first intercourse before the age of 16, 21.5% at age 16-17, 34.9% at age 18-19, 36.9% at age 20-24, and 5.1% at and age greater than or equivalent to 25.[2]

Contraception

* Contraception was restricted in the Irish Republic by the Censorship of Publications Act, 1929, and the Criminal Law Amendment Act, 1935 (reformed in 1979). Limited to medical prescription through pharmacies by the Health (Family Planning) Act, 1979, condoms were de-restricted (including vending machines) in June 1993.[3]
* Of 200 women obtaining abortions in Europe, 18% of single respondents used no method of contraception at first intercourse.[2] Of these women, the percentages who were using contraception at the time of pregnancy: 34.6% were using condoms, 28.4% were using withdrawal, 22.2% were using safe period, 7.4% were using the pill, 3.7% were using a diaphragm, 2.5% were using the IUD, and 1.2% were using a postcoital pill.[2]

Abortion

* Legislation: At the root of legislation is the 1861 (British) Offenses Against the Person Act, which makes providing "unlawful" abortions illegal. Due to the wording, this law is poorly defined and was used to back up earlier decisions to perform abortions in order to save the life of the woman.[4]
* In addition to this law, British parliament passed the Infant Life (Preservation) Act, which makes it unlawful to perform an abortion when the infant is capable of being born alive (28 weeks or more in gestational age), unless it is performed to save the life of the mother. This act was eventually enacted as the Criminal Justice (Northern Ireland) Act in 1945.[4]
* Since clarity was still lacking on these laws, in 1967 the Abortion Act was enacted in Britain which stated that abortions may be carried out, as deemed by two doctors, if the life of the mother, mentally or physically, is in danger, or of the infant will suffer serious mental or physical abnormalities or handicap after birth.[4]

* In the 1980s, the Right to Life movement was gaining power in Ireland, and they pushed until, in 1983, the Eighth Amendment to the Constitution of the Republic of Ireland was inaugurated, which absolutely made abortion illegal, unless the life of the mother is in danger.[4]

* In the interpretation of the law, the "respect' and "the right to life of the unborn," the anti-choice advocates in SPUC (Society for the Protection of the Unborn Child) in 1986 were able to prevent two counseling agencies for women from giving counseling about abortion. After appealing to the European Commission, these counseling agencies were allowed to open in 1991. However, a legal battle initiated by SPUC made the publication of any information about British abortion clinics was declared illegal and unconstitutional.[4] This was changed during the November 1992 referendum, and the provision of such information is now permitted.[5]

* In February 1992, a 14 year-old rape victim was prevented by the High Court to go to Britain to obtain an abortion. This led to a Supreme Court ruling allowing her to obtain an abortion, since her life was in danger due to suicide. Thus, in November, the freedoms to travel abroad and obtain information was approved.[5]

* Abortion is illegal in Ireland except in cases where the mother's life is in danger. Presently, an estimated 4,500 Irish women travel for abortions each year.[6]

* Backstreet abortions are not unknown, but their frequency is minimal given the safety valve of travel to Britain.[4]

Sex Education

* In Ireland, sex education does not exist in school curricula.[7]
* The Irish Family Planning Association (IFPA) has recently objected to a current Department of Health HIV/AIDS program in Irish schools, since students in most schools have not received education about sex, sexuality, physiology or relationships, and now, with the threat of HIV, they have suddenly only started talking about sex and death.[8]

STDs, Including AIDS[9]

* As of December, 1993, there have been 382 cases of AIDS reported.

Homosexuality

* In 1989 the Prohibition of Incitement to Hatred Act was enacted, making it illegal to incite hatred against lesbians and gay men.[10]
* In June 1993, despite strong opposition of the Roman Catholic Church, homosexual act between consenting males was made legal. The age of consent was set at 17, the same age for heterosexuals.[11] Lesbians are already covered by the consent laws.[12]
* In October 1993 the Employment Discrimination Law passed, which made it illegal to discriminate against employees on the basis of sexual preference.[10]
* Gays in the Military: No explicit legislation exists in this area. However, the Irish Minister of Defense has made it known that he would be in favor of outlawing discriminatory practices in relation to the employment of gays and lesbians in the army, and considers sexual orientation as an irrelevant factor in the performance of military duties.[13]

Prostitution[1]

* Prostitution is illegal.

Pornography[14]

* Pornography is illegal.

Resources

Irish Family Planning Association (IFPA), Unity Building (4th floor), 16/17 Lower O'Connell Street, Dublin 1, Ireland, Tel: (353 1) 878 0366, Fax: (353 1) 878 0375.

References

1. The World Sex Guide, "Prostitution in: Ireland," http://www.paranoia.com/faq/prostitution/Ireland.html, Last update: 1996/04/30, (C) 1994, 1995, 1996, Atta and M. <an48932@anon.penet.fi>, received 6/17/96.

2. Francome, "Irish Women Who Seek Abortions in England," Family Planning Perspectives (1992) vol. 24, No. 6, p. 265 & 266.

3. FPA Profile, "Irish Family Planning Association (IFPA) Ireland," Planned Parenthood in Europe, (1994) vol. 23, no. 1, p. 35.

4 Rolston & A. Eggert, Abortion in the New Europe A comparative Handbook, (Westport, CT, 1994) p. 159-169.

5. United Nations, Abortion Policies: A Global Review, vol. 2, 1992-<1993>, p. 68-70.

6. International Update, "Irish Court Asked to Rule on Right to Information on Abortion," Contemporary Sexuality, (1995) vol. 29, no. 5, p. 11.

7. Vilar, "School Sex Education: Still a Priority in Europe," Planned Parenthood in Europe, (1994), vol. 23, no.3, p. 9.

8. O'Brien, "Sexual Healthcare in Europe," Planned Parenthood in Europe, (1992), vol. 21, no. 1, p. 9

9. United Nations, Statistical Yearbook (NY 1995) p. 97.

10. Byrne, "Ireland-Legal Changes," Queer Resources Directory, Tue. 10 Jan 1995, http://abacus.oxy.edu/qrd/world/europe/ireland/gay.rights.progress-01.10.95, received 6/18/96.

11. Clarinet Communications Corp., Queer Resources Directory, http://abacus.oxy.edu/ qrd/world/europe/ireland/sodomy.repeal-6.24.93, received 6/18/96.

12. Bailey, The Pink Paper, London, "Ireland Moves to Legalize Gay Sex," Queer Resources Directory, http://abacus.oxy.edu/qrd/world/europe/ireland/sodomy. repeal. soon-IRELAND, received 6/18/96.

13. Dowling (pdowling@lib1.tcd.ie), "A: Employment By Private Companies," "Employment By the Government," & "B: Serving in the Military," Fri., 18 Mar 1994, http://abacus.oxy.edu/qrd/world/europe/ireland/summary.of.lgb.climate, received 6/18/96.

14. "Pornography: Restricted Access," http://www.pinkboard.com.au:80/r.html, received 6/19/96.

ISRAEL
POPULATION: 5 MILLION

Capital:
Jerusalem
(population: 567,100)

Major Cities & Populations: Tel Aviv-Jaffa 357,400; Haifa 246,500

Ethnic Groups: 83% Jewish; 17% non-Jewish (mostly Arab)

Languages: Official Languages: Hebrew and Arabic

Religions: 82% Jewish; 14% Muslim; 2% Christian

Annual Income per person: $11,330

Urban Population: 93%

Infant Mortality: 8 per 1,000 births

Life Expectancy: Females 78 years; Males 76 years

Literacy: 95%

Health Care System: Publicly funded health centers/clinics; 1 doctor per 345 people.

References:
The World Almanac and Book of Facts 1996(1995) Mahwah, NJ: World Almanac Books
Microsoft Home; Encarta Encyclopedia, Microsoft Corporation (1996). (CD- ROM).

Sexual Activity

* Typical age of first intercourse: 16 years old.[1]

Contraception

* No information available.

Abortion[2]

* Abortion has been allowed since 1952.
* An abortion must be performed by a physician in a recognized medical institution, with the written consent of the pregnant woman. A legal abortion requires the approval of a committee made up of two physicians and a social worker. The committee members must be appointed by the Director of the hospital where the abortion will be performed, or by the Minister of Health or a person appointed by him if the procedure is to be performed in another recognized medical institution.
* Abortions performed for medical reasons are paid for by the government; abortions performed on other grounds are paid for by the woman.

STD's, including AIDS

* There have been 446 cases of AIDS.[3]
* WHO estimates that 2,000 adults are HIV positive.[4]

Homosexuality

* Homosexuality is illegal in Israel, but no prosecution has ever been brought for the relationship between two consenting adults.[5]
* The army permits homosexuals to serve, but a 1993 directive cautions that they may be a security risk and should be checked on case by case; homosexuals are barred from top-secret jobs in army intelligence.[6]

Prostitution[7]

* Prostitution is legal in Israel. What is illegal is a second party making money off of this practice. Hence, pimping is illegal.
* Renting an apartment to a working girl is illegal because the rent is money made from prostitution.
* Massage and Escort services are illegal but usually not prosecuted.

Pornography

* Pornography in Israel is legal. Women are portrayed in magazines and on the street as objects. Cruelty in terms of degrading women sexually is seen as second nature to this country.[8]
* The legal age for viewing pornography in Israel is 18 years.[9]

Resources

* Institute for Sex Therapy. Sheba Medical Center, Tel Hashomer.
* Israel Family Planning Association. 9, Rambam Street, Tel-Aviv, 65601.
* Ministry of Education & Culture. Psychological and Counseling Services, 2 Devorah Hanevia Street, Jerusalem.

References

1. Birth Rates, Fertility Totals. http://www.odci.gov/cia/publications/9sfact/ja.html (retrieved 6/1 4/96).

2. United Nations, Abortion Policies: A Global Review (New York, 1992) p.71-73.

3. HIV.NET.   http://www.hiv.net (retrieved 6/18/96).

4. World Health Organization Global Programme on AIDS p.1-4 http://gpawww.who. ch/aidscase/dec/1995/hivtext.html   (retrieved 6/20/96)

5. Baedeker, S. Macmilion Travel: Israel (New York, 1995)

6. A. Riding, "In NATO, only U.S. & British Ban Gay Soldiers," The New York Times (Nov. 13, 1992) vol. 142, p. A12.

7. The World Sex Guide. Sun, June 4, 1995. http://www.paranoia. com/faq/prostitution/Israel.html   (retrieved   6/19/96).

8. A. Dworkin. "Israel: Whose Country Is It Anyway?" Ms. Magazine (Sept./Oct. 1990), vol. 1(2), p.68

9. Restricted Access.   http://www.pinkboard.com.au:80/r.html   (retrieved   6/19/96).

ITALY
POPULATION: 56.5 MILLION

Capital:
Rome (Roma)
(population: 2.8 million)

Major Cities & Populations:	Milan 1.4 million, Naples 1.2 million, Turin 1 million, Genoa 700,000, Palermo 700,000, Bologna 410,000, Florence 400,000
Ethnic Groups:	Lombards, Goths, Greeks, Saracens, Spaniards, Latins
Languages:	Italian, French, Fruilian, Slovene, German
Major Religions:	Roman Catholic (97.6%), Protestant
Income Per Capita:	$20,510
Urban Population:	70%
Infant Mortality:	7 per 1000 births
Life Expectancy:	Female 78 years, male 76 years
Adult Literacy:	97.1%
Health Care System:	National health plan, private hospitals

References:
Worldmark Encyclopedia of the Nations: Europe, Vol. 5, Eighth Edition, pp. 229-240,
   Gale Research Inc, Detroit, 1995.
The World Almanac and Book of Facts 1996 (1995), Mahwah, NJ: World Almanac Books

Sexual Activity

* The age of consent in Italy is 14.[1]
* People engaging in sexual relations with adolescents between the ages of 14 and 16 are punished if the younger person is a virgin, and if he/she reports the act. [1]
* 25% of high school students are sexually active, though uninformed about birth control and disease prevention. [2]

Contraception

* There has been a concern among legislators that induced abortion would become a method of family planning. Nevertheless, it has been mainly used as an emergency measure after the failure of contraceptives.[3]
* There is widespread ignorance in reproductive matters.[3]
* 45% would recommend the pill of IUD to a friend.[3]
* 32% of married women aged 18-44 use modern contraception.[4]
* Contraceptive use was legalized in 1971. Prior to that time, contraceptives were allowed only for medical reasons, though transgressions were tolerated.[5]
* 23% of women of reproductive age do not use any method of birth control.[5]
* 20% rely on withdrawal or rhythm methods.[5]
* Despite the low rates of contraceptive use, Italy has one of the lowest fertility rates in the world.[5]

Abortion

* Abortion is allowed for social, socio-economic, or socio-medical reasons up to 90 days.[6]
* It is allowed for medical or eugenic reasons, or because of rape or other sexual crimes only, after 90 days.[6]
* Women must have a doctor's certificate and wait at least one week.[6]
* Minors need parental permission.[6]
* Counseling is mandatory.[6]
* There is a considerable conscientious objection due to religious, moral or social reasons.[6]
* Illegal abortions are numerous.[6]
* Abortions are free of charge.[4]

* Medical personnel who are opposed to abortion can, in advance, declare their conscientious objection, and may be excused from performing abortions.[4]
* About 80% of women seeking abortion between 1983 and 1988 had been using contraception, although more than 70% were using the withdrawal method.[7]

Sex   Education

* Sex education is not provided in schools, and there are few family planning programs.[4]
* There is an interest in schools to implement sex education programs.[8]
* The government recently removed all references to condoms in its campaign against AIDS.[9]
* A 1991 survey of parents in Italy found that 83% discussed AIDS with their children, and 75% discussed sex.[10]
* 99% of parents believe that AIDS education should be taught in schools, and 91% believe that sex education should be taught in schools.[10]
* Parents feel that AIDS education should begin at an average age of 11.7 years, and sex education should begin at an average of 10.2 years.[10]
* 95% of parents feel that condoms should be used in AIDS education courses.[10]
* No more than 8% of parents opposed such education.[10]
* The Ministry of Health and the Ministry of Public Instruction have developed AIDS-education guidelines, and attempts have begun to increase HIV-prevention education in schools.[10]

STDs, including AIDS

* There have been more than 34,200 people diagnosed with AIDS in Italy, primarily IV drug users.[11]
* This is the third-highest rate in Europe.[11]
* There are 593 cases per million.[11]
* Police cannot keep criminals with AIDS in custody, as a 1992 decree stipulates that Italian prisoners with AIDS must be released from prison, but should remain under house arrest. Thousands of prisoners have been released under this law.[9]
* The average ages at diagnosis for IV drug users and heterosexuals have been 28 and 32 years, respectively.[10]
* Genital warts are the most frequently diagnosed STD with 30% of STD clinic patients infected.[11]

* Italy has a universal Hepatitis B vaccine program.[12]
* There are appoximately 9,000 deaths each year due to Hepatitis B, but this figure is slowly declining.[13]
* There are about 1.5 million Italians infected with Hepatitis B.[13]

Homosexuality

* Age of consent for homosexual and lesbai relations is 17.[14]
* National organization: ARCI GAY, headquartered in Bologna.[15]
* June 7, 1996, Pisa: homosexuals have equal legal and financial rights in long-term relationships.[15]
* Feb. 8, 1994, Verona: City council rejected European Parliament Resolution A3-0028/94 which called to end homosexual discrimination, to legitimize and equalize homosexual unions, to give homosexuals rights to adopt children, and to allow for endowment of gay and lesbian social organizations. The basis for this rejection was that "homosexuality contradicts Natural Law...and would have a negative effect upon the psychological development of young people...."[16]
* Proposals are being discussed to forbid lesbians from receiving artificial insemination.[17]
* Laws against "public indecency" and "obscenity prohibit homosexuals from hugging and kissing in public.[17]
* In Italy, homosexuals were excluded in the military until 1985, when the ban was lifted. Today, if a man admits that he is a homosexual, he is not required to serve in the military, though he may choose to do so.[18]

Prostitution[19]

* Prostitution is legal, but streetwalking and operating/working in a brothel are not.
* Prostitutes are not registered. No health check ups are required.
* Soliciting a prostitute is illegal. (This law has been used against husbands and boyfriends of prostitutes.)
* Minors engaging in prostitution are institutionalized.
* There are many small brothels.
* There is widespread streetwalking.
* Call girls, known as "squillo" work out of their own apartments, advertising in local papers.

Pornography[20]

* Legal age for viewing pornography is 18 years.

Resources

*Associazione per la Ricerca in Sessuologia (ARS), Via Angelo Cappi 1/8. II 16126 Genova
*Centro Italiano di Sessuologia, Via della Lungarina, 65, Rome, 00153.
*Instituto di Sessuologia di Savona, 17026 Noli, Via la Malfa, 5, Savona
*Unione Italiana Educazione Matrimoniale e Prematrimoniale (UICEMP), Via Eugenio Chiesa 1, 20122 Milan

References

1. "Age-Of-Consent Laws of the World," <http://www.c2.org/`prd/world/acc.html> 6/19/96.
2. "Attitudes of Parents of High School Students About AIDS, Drug, and Sex Education in Schools--Rome, Italy, 1991," JAMA, April 22/29, 1992, Vol 297, No. 16, p. 2160
3. "Induced Abortion and Contraception in Italy," Planned Parenthood in Europe, Vol. 20, No. 2, 1991.
4. Abortion Policies, A Global Review, Vol. II, p. 74-76, United Nations, NY 1992.
5. Maragarita Delgado Perez, Massimo Livi-Bacci, "Fertility in Italy and Spain: The Lowest in the World," Family Planning Perspectives, Vol. 24, No. 4, July/August, 1992, pp. 162-171.
6. National Abortion Campaign, "Abortion Laws in Europe," (amended Jan 1995), London, England.
7. Angela Spinelli and Michelle E. Grandolfo, "Induced Abortion and Contraception in Italy," Planned Parenthood in Europe, Vol. 20, No. 2, p. 18-19, 1991.
8. Duarte Vilar, "School Sex Education: Still a Priority in Europe," Planned Parenthood in Europe, Vol. 23, No. 3, p. 8, 1994.
9. AASECT, Contemporary Society, 10/95, Vol. 29, No. 10, P. 7.
10. HIV.NET, http://www.hiv.net, 6/19/96
11. B. Suligoi, M. Giuliani, N. Binkin. The National STD Surveillance System in Italy: Results of the First Year of Activity." International Journal for STDs and AIDS. March-April, 1994, pp. 93-100.
12. C. Roure. "Overview of Epidemiology and Disease Burden of Hepatitis B in the European Region." Vaccine, 1995, vol. 13, Supplement 1, pp. 18-21.
13. P. Crovari, "Epidemiology of Viral Hepatitis B in Italy." Vaccine, 1995, Supplement pp. 18-21.
14. Alan F. Reekie, "Age of Consent Laws in the Council of Europe States in 1993," <http://ftp.tcp.com/qrd/world/europe/age.of.consent.laws-12.20.94>.
15. <Http://www.qrd.org/qrd/world/europe/italy/equal.rights.news-03.21.94.>
16. "Motion, The Verona City Council," (translated by Jude R. Montarsi), <http://www.qrd.org/qud/world/europe/italy/verona.council-action.alert, 6/12/96>.
17. Alexandra Duda, "Comparative Survey of the Legal and Societal Situation of Homosexuals in Europe" (updated version), <http://www.quality.org/FQRD/ilga/euroletter/35-Survey.html>, 8/95.
18. Alan Riding, New York Times, 1992, v. 142, Nov. 13, p. A 12, Col. 4.
19. World Sex Guide, "Prostitution in: Italy," <http://www.paranoia.com/faq/prostitution/Italy.html>, 6/19/96.
20. Restricted Access, <http://www.pinkboard.com.au:80/r.html>, 6/19/96.

JAPAN
POPULATION: 126 MILLION

Capital:
Tokyo
(population: 8 million)

Major Cities & Populations: Yokohama 3.3 million; Osaka 2.6 million; Nagoya 2.2 million

Ethnic Groups: 99% Japanese; 1% Other including Koreans, Chinese, and Ainu

Languages: Official Language: Japanese

Major Religions: Buddhism, Shintoism shared by large majority

Annual Income Per Person: $26,920

Urban Population: 78%

Infant Mortality 4 per 1,000 births

Life Expectancy: Females 82 years; Males 77 years

Literacy: 100%

Health Care System: The combination of public and private funding has created the insurance pension system needed for the hospitals, clinics and physicians.

References:
The World Almanac and Book of Facts 1996(1995) Mahwah, NJ: World Almanac Books
Microsoft Home; Encarta Encyclopedia, Microsoft Corporation (1996). (CD- ROM).

Sexual Activity[1]

* Japanese culture has strongly urged young people, particularly girls, to wait until marriage to have sex.
* While a quarter of US girls and a third of US boys have had sex by the age of 15, in Japan it is just 4% for girls and 6% for boys by this age.

Contraception[2]

* The government has limited access to birth control pills as part of a strategy to encourage condom use that will eliminate the spread of HIV. The pill can be obtained by Japanese doctors for treatment of menstrual disorders, but not used for birth control.
* Presently Japan is the only industrialized nation that bans "the pill."
* Historical factors have caused individuals in Japan to rely on condoms, rhythm method, and abortion for fertility control.

Abortion

* Legal restrictions were lifted in 1948, legalizing abortion in the first 5 months of pregnancy. All legal abortions must be performed within medical facilities at the compliance of a physician assigned by a local medical association. When the pregnancy is a result of rape or incest, the abortion can be performed without the legal consent of the woman.[3]
* Japan has an average of 300,000 to 400,000 abortions per year.[4]

Sex Education

* Sex education in schools is mandated beginning at age 10 or 11; it typically focuses on reproductive issues.[1]
* Guidelines for HIV/AIDS education in schools:[5]
  1) As a part of hygiene education, all grade schools must teach students that HIV is a blood-borne infection.
  2) Middle schools will teach students about HIV/AIDS in the context of other sexually transmitted diseases.
  3) High schools are permitted to mention condoms as protection against HIV infection.
* The Ministry of Education believes that teachers should teach HIV/AIDS prevention to students without mentioning sexual intercourse.[5]

STD, including AIDS[6]

* AIDS cases reported to date: 889
* WHO estimates that 8,678 adults are HIV positive.

Homosexuality[7]

* Japan does not have an exclusive policy regarding gays in the military.

Prostitution[8]

* Prostitution is illegal, as is visiting a prostitute, but the two are not punishable.

Pornography

* The legal age for viewing pornography in Japan is 18 years.[9]
* The Japanese government has proposed to set up an independent search to control the transmission of obscene or criminal material over the Internet.[10]

Resources

* Japan Institue for Research in Education. 4-3-6-702 Kozimachi Chiyodaku, Tokyo 7102.
* Japanese Association for Sex Education. (JASE). Miyata Bldg. 1-3 Kanada Jinbocho, Chiyoda-Ku, Tokyo 101.
* Japnase Association of Sex Educators, Counselors and Therapists (JASECT), JASE Clinic, 3F Shin-Anoyama Bldg. (West), 1-1 Minami, Aoyama, 1-chome Minato-Ku, Tokyo 107.
* Japanese Organization for Interantional Cooperation in Family Planning, Inc. (JOIC~). 1-1, Ichigaya Sadohara-cho, Shinjuku-ku, Tokyo 107.

References

1. G. Kelly, Sexuality Today (Guilford, CT: Brown & Benchmark, 1996) p. 247.

2. "Japan To Keep Banning Pill," Contemporary Sexuality (AASECT, May 1992), vol. 26(5), p. 6.

3. United Nations, Abortion Policies: A Global Review (New York, 1992) p.79-81.

4. "Japanese Practice Mourning Ritual for Abortions," Contemporary Sexuality (AASECT, March 1996), vol. 30(3), p. 4.

5. K. Kitazawa, "Sexuality Issues inJapan," SIECUS Report (Dec 1993/Jan 1994) p.7-11.

6. World Health Organization, Global Programme on AIDS. p. 1-4 http://gpawww.who.ch/aidscase/dec/1995/hivtext.html (retrieved 6/17/96).

7. S. Harris, "Military Policies Regarding Homosexual Behavior: An International Survey." Journal of Homosexuality (1991), vol. 21(4), p .67-74.

8. Prostitution In Japan." The World Sex Guide. http://www.paranoia.com/faq/prostitution/Japan.html (retrieved 6/18/96)

9. Restricted Access. http://www.pinkboard.com.au:80/r.html (retrieved 6/19/96).

10. "Governments Crack Down On The Internet," Information Society Trends Issues (December 2, 1996) Editorial.

KENYA
POPULATION: 28.8 MILLION

Capital:
Nairobi
(population: 959,000)

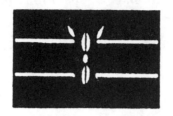

Major Cities & Populations: Nairobi 959,000; Mombasa 401,000

Ethnic Groups: Kikuyu 21%; Luhya 14%; Luo 13%
Kamba 11%; Kalenjin 11%

Languages: Swahili & English (official), Kikuyu, Luhya, Luo, Kimeru and others

Major Religions: Roman Catholic 28%; Protestant 26%; Traditional Beliefs 18%; Islam 6%

Annual Income per Person: $340

Urban Population: 27%

Infant Mortality: 73 per 1,000 live births

Life Expectancy: Female 54 years; male 51 years

Adult Literacy: 69%, 80% male, 59% female

Health Care System: Provided by government, private individuals, churches and voluntary services; 1 doctor per 7,410 people

References:
Encyclopedic World Atlas (1994) NY: Oxford University Press
Kenya http://www.care.org/world/profiles/kenya.html 6/10/96
Kenya http://www.rcbowen.com/kenya/health.html 6/11/96
The World Almanac and Book of Facts 1996 (1995) Mahwah, NJ: World Almanac Books

Sexual Activity

* Adolescent women represent up to 20 percent of the country's total fertility rate of 6.7, most women have their first child before age 18.[1]
* First sexual contact can be as early as 10-12 in both boys and girls; sexuality has a lot to do with culture, education, family units and economic factors.[2]
* Young men frequent prostitutes, often for their first sexual encounter.[1]
* Young girls who become pregnant are expelled from school.[1]
* A study done in 1987 estimated 8,000 girls dropped out of schools (both primary and secondary) due to pregnancy (8.6 per 1,000).[1]
* Most abortions performed on teenagers and women under the age of 25.[2]

Contraception

* Culture and religious beliefs prohibit the use on contraception.[2]
* Kenya has had a low contraceptive use rate.[3]
* There is general knowledge about contraception among youths, but little practical information[2] and much misinformation about side effects hinder the introduction to modern contraceptives.[1]
* Government is reluctant to teach adolescents about contraception, or provide it to unmarried women.[2]
* Pills, IUDs, injectables and "natural planning" are methods currently used,[4] with injectables being the preferred method because they are easily hid from their men.[5]
* Only 12% of Kenyan men currently use condoms.[6]

Abortion

* Abortion is illegal unless the mother's life is at risk.[7]
* In 1993, at least 187,500 pregnancies ended in abortion, of these 75,000 were induced.[2]
* Induced abortion is not an uncommon experience, especially among young, single, urban women.[7]
* Women believe abortion is a "woman's issue", and that of a man's is only pressure when the pregnancy is unwanted.[7]
* Information about abortion services is readily available through friends or friends of friends.[7]
* Cost of abortions vary considerably, from as low as $36 to $162 for one performed in a hospital or private clinic; abortions performed within the community ranged from no charge to $22.50 performed in a private house.[7]

Sex   Education

* Sexuality and other issues related to family life are passed on to them through family-based education and guidance.[1]
* A study, done by Ajayi et al., 1991, found that 68 percent of 3,000 youth aged 12-19 surveyed had received some information on sexuality, with school, friends and same sex relatives.[1]
* In absence of traditional sources of information, young people turn to their peers for information concerning issues relating to sex.[1]
* Many schools are run by religious orders, and the government opposes sex education in the school.[2]

STDs,   including   AIDS

* Youth are largely aware of STDs including HIV/AIDS, but often misinformed on modes of transmission and which diseases are actually sexually transmitted.[1]
* By 2010, the average lifespan in Kenya will be 40, due to AIDS.[8]
* 1 in 26 persons is HIV positive.[9]
* 80% of HIV infection is due to heterosexual sex and 20 percent due to male-male sex.[8]
* AIDS more prevalent among higher paid workers because of traveling to big cities to find work.[10]

Homosexuality

* Kenya criminalizes sex between two people of the same sex.[11]
* Homosexuality is prohibited under the country's laws and is morally unacceptable to society.[12]

Prostitution

* Most young men visit prostitutes for their first sexual experience.[1]
*In an economy with too few jobs, single women without education are turning to prostitution.[13]
* A great number of women in the cities who have been abandoned by men or in need of extra income also turn to prostitution.[9]
* Youth seem to know the price of an encounter ($0.50 US) and the locations where to find them.[1]

Pornography

* No information available.

Resources

*Family Planning Private Sector Programme, Fifth Floor, Longonot Place, Kijabe Street, P.O. Box 46042, Nairobi.
*International Planned Parenthood Federation-Kenya, Box 30234, Nairobi, Kenya

References

1 G. Barker and S. Rich, (1992, May/June).   Influences on adolescent sexuality in Nigeria and Kenya: Findings from recent focus-group discussions, Studies in Family Planning Vol. 23 (n3), pp. 199-210.

2. D. Lorch, (1995, June 4), Unsafe abortions become a big problem in Kenya, The New York Times Vol. 144, p. 3(N).

3. United Nations, Abortion policy: A global review Vol. 1, (New York, 1992), pp. 87-88.

4. A. Ferguson, (1992, July/August).   Fertility and contraceptive adoption and discontinuation in rural Kenya, Studies in Family Planning Vol. 23 (n4), pp. 257-267.

5. J. Ozanne, (1990, July).   Kenya fights its baby boom, World Press Review Vol. 37 (n7), p. 67.

6. D. Lorch, (1993, Dec. 18).   After years of ignoring AIDS epidemic, Kenya has begun facing up to it, The New York Times Vol. 143, p. 5.

7. J. Baker and S. Khasiani, (1992, January/February).   Induced abortion in Kenya: Case histories, Studies in Family Planning Vol. 23, (n1), pp. 34-44.

8. Rex Wockner, (1995, Dec. 14).   Grim AIDS predictions from Africa, http://www.qrd.org/qrd/world/wockner/news.briefs/085-12.14.95,   06/18/96.

9. International Update, Contemporary Sexuality, July 1996, p. 6.

10. D. Lorch, (1993, Dec. 18).   After years of ignoring AIDS epidemic, Kenya has begun facing up to it, The New York Times Vol. 143, p. 5.

11. Tielman and Hammelburg, The Third Pink Book: A Global View of Lesbian and Gay Liberation and Oppression, (1993), Buffalo, NY: Prometheus Books.

12. Rex Wockner, (1994, Nov. 3).   Kenya deports homosexual, http://www.qrd.org/qrd/world/wockner/news.briefs/027-11.03.94,   06/18/96.

13. S. Okie, (1993, Dec. 14).   An AIDS clue in Kenya?, The Washington Post Vol. 117, p. WH9.

MEXICO
(UNITED MEXICAN STATES)
POPULATION: 94 MILLION

Capital:
Mexico City
(population: 18.5 million)

Major Cities & Populations: Mexico City 18,.5 million; Guadalajara 2.6 million; Monterrey 2.3 million; Puebla de Zaragoza 1.2 million

Ethnic Groups: Mestizo 60%, Amerindian 30%, Caucasian 9%

Languages: Spanish (official) & various Mayan dialects

Major Religions: Roman Catholic 89%, Protestant 6%

Annual Income per Person: $2,870

Urban Population: 73%

Infant Mortality: 36 per 1,000 live births

Life Expectancy: Females 74 years; Males 67 years

Adult Literacy: 90%

Health Care System: Social welfare

References:
CIA 1995 Fact Book, (retrieved July 6, 1996) http://www.odci.gov/cia/publications/ 95fact/mx.html
Europa World Year Book 1995, Vol II, Europa Publications Limited, London:1995.
Rayner, Caroline, ed., Encyclopedic World Atlas, Oxford University Press, NY:1994.

Sexual Activity

* The legal age of consent is 21.[1]
* The median age for first intercourse is rising among Mexico's women. For women age 45-49, the age of first intercourse was 18.9; for women age 20-24, it was 19.8.[2]
* In Mexico City, almost 2/3 of women aged 18-19 with premarital sexual experience have been pregnancy at least once.[2]

Contraception

* 55% of married women (aged 15-49) use modern contraception.[3]
* 11% of married women of reproductive age use IUD's.[3]
* Oral contraceptives are sold without a prescription; emergency contraception is implicitly available without a prescription.[4]
* The number of complaints of forced sterilization rose in 1995. Most were performed in public hospitals on poor and illiterate women who were not advised of the consequences of the medical procedure. While the 1984 General Health Law makes it a crime to pressure women to have sterilization procedures without their consent, very few charges have been brought.[5]
* As of 1987, 19% of married women of reproductive age were sterilized. The procedure is free upon request in government clinics and hospitals.[6]
* 60% of women who seek State sponsored birth control do so without the knowledge of their husband.[7]

Abortion

* The Decree of 2 January 1931, as amended 16 February 1971, makes abortion illegal except in cases of medical or legal grounds to save the life of the woman or in cases of rape or incest. Some interpretations allow abortion in order to preserve the physical health of the woman, although this interpretation varies from state to state.[8]
* Most abortions are performed during the first trimester. They must be performed by a physician with the corroboration of another physician as to the necessity of the procedure. The consent of the woman and her husband (or in the case of teens, a parent or guardian) is required.[8]
* It is estimated that 42% of women having induced abortions have complications.[9]

Sex Education[10]

* It is the government's policy to stabilize population growth. To that end, the Population Law of January 1974 gave power to the Secretary of Government to implement family planning by means of education and services to the public, while the Sanitary Code of 1973 (Sec. 34) provides for family planning in schools.
* Article 4 of the Constitution guarantees citizens the right to family planning information.
* Publicity for contraception is allowed, but rare.
* The conservative Catholic Church opposes sex education. As of 1974, students resented sexology with family planning as imperialistic.

STDs, including AIDS

* As of December, 1995, there were 220,000 AIDS cases reported in Mexico.[11]
* The increase in reported AIDS cases is paralleling the rate found in the United States in 1987.[12]
* Most cases of AIDS are found in homosexual or bisexual males.[12]
* Most cases of AIDS in women are contracted through blood or derivatives. Less than 1% are contracted via intravenous drug use, 6% through perinatal contact, and 28% through heterosexual contact.[12]
* Most bi-sexual men do not use condom when having sex with women.[12]

Homosexuality[5]

* The Mexican Constitution states that men and women are equal. Education should promote the ideals of "fraternity and equal rights of all mankind, avoiding privileges of race, sects, groups, sexes or individuals." This law is not effectively enforced. Amnesty International cites Mexico homosexual men and women to be the most likely victims of abuse and violence.
* At least twelve homosexual and nine male prostitutes were killed in Juxtla Gutierrezx between 1991 and 1993.
* Discrimination against homosexuals in hiring and promotion is widespread.

Prostitution[13]

* Larger cities have "zona roja" where prostitution is allowed. Prostitutes are registered, get health checks and must carry a card to prove it.
* Cab drivers know the locations of prostitutes and will drive customers to those locations and wait for them.
* Liboria Cruz, a 19 year old male prostitute, was beaten by a group of men in Mexico City in June, 1995.

Pornography[13]

* The hardest pornography openly available is equivalent to *Hustler* or *Penthouse*.
* Video stores carry pornographic movies, but don't display the boxes.

Resources

*Fundacion Mexican Para la Planeacion Familiar (MEXFAM), Calle Juarez 208, Tlalpan, 14000 Mexico City, DF, Mexico. Tel: (5) 573-7348
*National AIDS Committee, Secretary for Health, Lieja Numero 7, Col. Juarez, 1er Piso, 04360 Mexico City, DF, Mexico. Tel: (5) 554-9112
*International Gay and Lesbian Association-Mexico (Associacion Lesbia y Gay Internacional-Mexico), Apartado Postal 1-1693, 06030 Mexico City, DF, Mexico
*Academy of Human Rights, Apartado Postal 78282, CD Universitaria, 04510, Mexico City, DF, Mexico

References

1. "Legal Age of Consent." <http://www.pinkboard.com.au/consent.html>   updated June 10, 1996. (retrieved June 27, 1996).

2. A. McCauley, "Meeting the Needs of Young Adults," Population Reports, Series J, October 1995, No. 41, Baltimore: Johns Hopkins University.

3. K. Treiman, "IUDs - An Update," Population Reports, Series B, December 1995, No. 6. Baltimore: Johns Hopkins University.

4. United Nations, World Abortion Policies 1994, Department for Economic and Social Information and Policy Analysis, Population Division, New York, 1994. <gopher: //gopher.undp.org:70/00/ungophers/popin/wdtrends/charts.asc> (retrieved June 19, 1996).

5. Gopher://dosfan.lib.uic.edc:70/OF - 1%3a23367%3AMexico.

6. C. Church, "Voluntary Sterilization: Number One and Growing," Population Reports, Series C, November 1990, No. 10, Baltimore: Johns Hopkins University.

7. G. Kelly, Sexuality Today (Guilford, CT: Brown & Benchmark, 1995), p. 514.

8. United Nations, Abortion Policies: A Global Review, New York, 1993, p. 142-143.

9. C. Ellertson, "Expanding Access to Emergency Contraception in Developing Countries. Studies in Family Planning, 1995, vol. 26(5), p. 256.

10. E. Kellogg, World's Laws and Practices on Population and Sexuality Education, Medford, 1975.

11. WHO, "Provisional Working Estimates of Adult HIV Prevalence as of end of 1995 by country." <http://gpa.who.ch/aidscase/dec1995/hivtext.html> (retrieved June 24, 1996.)

12. M. Hernandez, Sexual Behavior and Status for HIV Type 1 among Homosexual and Bisexual Males in Mexico City, American Journal of Epidemiology, 1995, Vol. 135(8).

13. The World Sex Guide. <an48932@anon.penet.fi>   http://www.paranoia.com/faq/ prostitution/Mexico.html, last updated April 30, 1996. (retrieved June 21, 1996).

NETHERLANDS
POPULATION: 15.5 MILLION

Capital:
Amsterdam
(Population: 700,500)

Major Cities & Populations: Amsterdam: 700,500; Rotterdam: 596,000; The Hague: 445,000

Ethnic Groups: Dutch 96%, Moroccans, Turks,& other 4%

Languages: Dutch

Major Religions: Roman Catholic 34%, Protestant 25% Muslim 3%, other 2%, unaffiliated 36%

Annual Income per Person: $18,000

Urban Population: 89%

Infant mortality: 6 per 1,000 births

Life Expectancy: Females: 81 yrs. Males: 75 yrs.

Adult Literacy: 100%

Health Care System: Hospitals and private physicians

References:
1995 CIA World FactBook.
1993 Grolier Electronic Publishing, Inc.
1992 World Population Reference Bureau.

121

Sexual Activity

* Legal age of consent for sex: Male-Female: 12/16, Male-Male: 12/16, Female-Female: 12/16 (Two ages are shown: sexual activity is legal at the lower age unless the younger person subsequently complains.)[1]
* 51% of girls aged 16-19 have had sexual intercourse.[2]

Contraception

* Oral contraception, as well as other 'medical' methods of contraception have been available free of charge in The Netherlands since 1972.[3]
* Emergency contraception, commonly known as "the morning after pill," has been available since the 1960's.[4]
* The most popular methods of contraception are: The Pill 39%; Sterilization (male or female): 21% ; I.U.D.: 3%; Condom: 6.5%; No contraception: 28%.[5]
* "Double Dutch" - the use if the Pill and condom together for protection from pregnancy and diseases - is popular in the Netherlands.[4]

Abortion[5]

* Abortion is available on request if woman is in situation of emergency.[7]
* Menstrual regulation is available up to 16 days from missed period (20% of all abortions).
* The Netherlands has the lowest abortion rate in Europe: 4 abortions per 1000 among teens.
* Consultation with a doctor followed by a five day waiting period is necessary before an abortion is performed.
* Approximately 80% of abortions are performed before the 8th week of pregnancy, only 1.3% after the 15th week.

Sex Education[6]

* There is no government provision to include sex education, but sex education is available at all levels of school education.
* Sex education is also available through youth clubs, evening classes for adults and is also covered by the mass media.

STD's, including AIDS

* AZT is the only antiviral drug aprroved for HIV.[7]
* There have been 3,000 cases of AIDS, 36% of adult prevalence rate. [8]

Homosexuality

* The Dutch Parliament favors gay marriages, allowing gay couples many of the same rights as that of straight married couples but without the right to adopt children.[9]
* In 1974, there was an abolition of the ban on gays in the military[10]

Prostitution[11]

* Prostitution is legal.
* Since 1988 it has been defined as a legal profession with its own union sector.
* Prostitutes are not registered nor required to get health checks.
* Pimping and facilitating prostitution is illegal.
* The age of consent is 16.

Pornography[12]

* The legal age for viewing pornographic materials is 18.

Resources

*Dutch Centre for Health Promotion & Health Education, P.O. Box 5104, 3502 JC Utrecht
*Netherlands Institute of Social Sexological Research (NISSO), P.O. Box 5018, 3052 JA Utrecht
*Rutgers Stitching, Oudenoord 170, 3515 EV Utrecht, The Netherlands, Tel: (31 30) 231 3431; Fax: (31 30) 231 9387.

References

1. PinkBoard HomePage: "Legal Age of Consent"
   <http://www.pinkboard.com.au/consent.html>

2. E. Ketting: "Is the Dutch Abortion Rate Really That Low?" Planned Parenthood in Europe (1994) Vol. 23, No. 3, p. 29-32.

3. H. Doppenberg: "Free Pill in The Netherlands: For How Much Longer?" Planned Parenthood in Europe (1994), Vol. 23, No. 1, p. 8-9.

4. Transcript from: "Dutch Treat" NBC 20\20 episode, Jan. 1995.

5. B. Rolston, A. Eggert, editors. Abortion in the New Europe: A Comparative Handbook (Westport, CT: 1994) table II, p. xxvi

6. P. Meredith & L. Thomas (editors) Planned Parenthood in Europe: A Human Rights Perspective, (1986) p. 100.

7. Act Up! Amsterdam: "What a Small Country Can Be Big In: Hypocrisy"
   <http://gopher.hivnet.org:70/0/hivtext3/actup-e>

8. World Health Organization, Global programme on AIDS, December 1995,
   <http://gpawww.who.ch/aidscase/dec1995/hivtext.html>

9. Dutch Gay News: "Dutch Parliament Favours Gay Marriage" February 1996,
   <http://www.xs4all.nl/~berts/dg960226.html#top>

10. R. Janssen, "Gays in Dutch Army" Europe. (1993), No. 325, April, pg. 37.

11. World Sex Guide, Prostitution in The Netherlands: last update: 1996.
    <http://www.paranoia.com/faq/prostitution/Netherlands.html>

12. Restricted Access <http://www.pinkboard.com.au:80/r.html>
    <panther@pinkboard.com.au>

NEW ZEALAND
POPULATION: 3.5 MILLION

Capital:
Wellington
(population: 329,000)

Major Cities & Populations:	Auckland, 929,300; Wellington, 329,000; Christchurch 318,100; Hamilton 153,800
Ethnic Groups:	White 81%; Maori 9%; Polynesian 3%
Languages:	English (official), Maori
Major Religions:	Anglican 24%; Presbyterian 18%; Roman Catholic 15%; Methodist 5%; Baptist 2%
Annual Income per Person:	$12,140
Urban Population:	85%
Infant Mortality:	9 per 1,000 births
Life Expectancy:	Female 79 years; male 73 years
Adult Literacy:	99%
Health Care System:	70% publicly funded, with private physicians and clinics bridging gap in waiting time for non-emergency services; mid-wifery fully subsidized

References:
CIA 1995 Fact Book, http://www.odci.gov/cia/publications/95fact/nz.html
Health care,http://www-leland.stanford.edu/~jmgeorge/health.html
New Zealand Official Yearbook 95. (Auckland: Statistics New Zealand, 1995).
New Zealand: The People, http://www.govt.nz/ps/min/stats/nzpeople.html#Births
Rayner, Caroline, ed., Encyclopedic World Atlas, Oxford Univ. Press, New York:1994.

Sexual Activity

* Age for sexual consent is 16 years old.[1]
* The rising rate of teen pregnancy is a growing public issue.[2]

Contraception

* Age of consent for medical treatment is as low as 14 in parts of New Zealand.[3]
* Indirect support is provided by the governmentally run health program.[4]
* 62% of married women use modern contraception.[5]
* The Pill and female sterilization are the most popular methods.[6]
* Less than 5% of married women of reproductive age use IUDs.[3]

Abortion

* Abortion is available to women in their first trimester, from regular physicians in licensed institutions. The procedure is free if performed at a public hospital. After the first trimester, abortions are available within an institution with "full license," and with the approval of a committee of three: two certifying physicians, one of which is an OB/GYN, and the operating surgeon. Counseling of the mother is a prerequisite.[2]
* Abortions can be obtained in order to save the woman's life, to preserve the physical or mental health of the mother, in cases of rape or incest, fetal impairment or for economic or social reasons.[5]

Sex Education

* Family planning information is available from family physicians, private specialists and clinics to help clients make informed and responsible choices regarding reproductive and sexual health.[7]
* A study by Rosser shows that teaching safer sex using tactics of fear, monogamy or abstinence increases the incidence of unsafe sex in high risk individuals and so increases the spread of HIV. The study also shows that anti-discrimination legislation and teaching of tolerance of homosexuality helps decrease the spread of AIDS.[8]

STDs, including AIDS

* In 1993, a law was passed which bans discrimination because of the presence of disease, including HIV and Hepatitis.[9]
* 12,000 AIDS cases have been reported as of December, 1995.[10]

Homosexuality

* Prior to the 1986 Homosexual Law Reform Act, homosexuality was illegal with penalties of up to two years imprisonment.[9]
* The 1993 Human Rights Act includes sexual orientation as one of the grounds on which discrimination is not allowed.[9]
* Some health care providers are concerned that because of the 1993 Human Rights Act, they can't refuse treatment from gay couples for assisted human reproduction.[11]
* Homosexual behavior is considered a psychiatric problem. There is cultural disapproval for at least some form of homosexual behavior.[12]
* The military excludes gays from military service.[12]
* Homosexuals, along with the disabled and psychiatric patients, have been granted protection from discrimination in jobs, housing, education and provision of goods. The Homosexual Law Reform Act passed by a margin of 5 votes. A clause banning discrimination because of sexual orientation was dropped because of strong opposition.[9]

Prostitution[13]

* Prostitution is legal and is advertised, even on the radio.
* Ads appear in magazine for girls and organizations that arrange calls for $90-120 with all sex included. Prostitutes can be found through ads for escorts or massage parlors in the telephone yellow pages

Pornography[7]

* The Films, Videos and Publications Act of 1993 covers publications of all types (audio/visual, written, or computerized). The legislation calls for levels of classification: unrestricted is labeled green and is available to anyone; unrestricted with a yellow label is available only to certain ages; restricted is given a red label and is available to certain ages; objectionable "describes, depicts or otherwise deals with matters such as sex, horror, crime, cruelty or violence...to be injurious to the public good."

Resources

*New Zealand Family Planning Association (NZPFA), Dixon House, Castrol Street, Wellington, NZ. Tel: (4) 384-4349

*Pregnancy Counselling Services, PO Box 33-423, Takapuna, Auckland, NZ. Tel: (9) 489-6505

*National Council on AIDS, AIDFS Task Force, Department of Health, PO Box 5013, Wellington, NZ. Tel: (4) 496-2179

*Abortion Law Reform Assoc. of New Zealand (ALRANZ), PO Box 28-008, Kelburn, Wellington 5, NZ. Tel: (4) 475-7665

*New Zealand Prostitutes Collective, PO Box 11-412, 282 Cuba Street, Wellington, NZ. Tel: (4) 382-8791

*Women against Pornography, PO Box 11-874, Wellington, NZ. Tel: (4) 384-6340

*Society for the Protection of the Unborn Childl - New Zealand, Box 12-286, Thorndon, Wellington, NZ. Tel: (4) 472-1451

*Women for Life, PO Box 26-142, Epsom, Auckland, NZ. Tel: (9) 523-3992

Reference

1. Alan F. Reekie, "Age of Consent Laws in the Council of Europe States in 1993," <http://ftp.tcp.com/qrd/world/europe/age.of.consent.laws-12.20.94>.
2. United Nations, <u>Abortion Policies: A Global Review</u>, Vol II, Department for Economic and social Information and Policy Analysis, New York, 1993.
3. A. Mcauley, "Meeting the Needs of Young Adults," <u>Population Reports</u>, Series J, No. 41, Baltimore: Johns Hopkins School of Public Health, Population Information Program, October 1995.
4. W. Dynes, <u>Encyclopedia of Homosexuality</u>, Vol. II New York: Guilford, 1990, p. 473.
5. Department for Economic and Social Information and Policy Analysis Population Division, <u>World Abortion Policies 1994</u>, (New York: United Nations, 1994. <gopher://gopher.undp.org:70/00/ungophers/popin/wdtrends/charts.asc> (retrieved June 18, 1996).
6. E. Jamison, <u>World Population Profile: 1994</u>, U.S. Department of Commerce Economics and Statistical Administration, Bureau of Census, Washington, D.C. 1994, p. A-42.
7. <u>New Zealand Official Yearbook 95</u>, Auckland, Statistics New Zealand: 1995.
8. B. Rosser, Male Homosexual Behavior and the Effects of AIDS Education: A. Study of Behavior and Safer Sex in New Zealand and Southern Australia, Praeger, 1991.
9. "New Zealand Bans Discrimination," <u>The Dominion</u>, Wellinton, NZ: July 29, 1993.
10. Provisional Working Estimates of Adult HIV Prevalence as of end of 1995 by Country, WHO, <http://gpa.who.ch/aidscase/dec1995/hivtext.html> (retrieved June 24, 1996).
11. K. Daniels, "Review of the New Zealand Gov ernment Report into Assisted Human Reproduction (AHR), <u>Eugios Ethics Institute Newsletter 4</u>, 1994, <http://www.biol.tsukuba.as.jp/~macer/EEIN45C.html>. (retrieved June 13, 1996).
12. S. Harris, "Miltiary Policies Regarding Homosexual Behavior: An International Survey," <u>Journal of Homosexuality</u>, 1991, Vol 21 (4).
13. <u>The World Sex Guide</u>. <an48932@anon.penet.fi> http://www.paranoia.com/faq/prostitution/Mexico.html, last updated April 30, 1996. (retrieved June 21, 1996).

NORWAY
POPULATION: 4,330,951

Capital:
Oslo
(population: 726,000)

Major Cities & Populations: Bergen 211,000; Trondheim 136,000; Stavanger 101,403

Ethnic Groups: Germanic: Nordic, Alpine, Baltic; Lapps (Sami)

Languages: Norwegian (official)

Major Religions: Evangelical Lutheran 87.8%; other Protestant & Roman Catholic

Annual Income Per Person: $22,170

Urban Population: 76%

Infant Mortality: 6 per 1,000

Life Expectancy: Female 81 years; Male 74 years

Adult Literacy: 99%

Health Care: There are 2,248 doctors, 881 dentists, 724 pharmacists, and 8,465 nurses per 1 million people. There are 6 hospital beds per 1,000 people.

References:
Encyclopedic World Atlas (1994) NY: Oxford University Press.
The World Almanac and Book of Facts 1996 (1995) Mahwah, NJ: World Almanac Books

Sexual Activity

* Legal age of consent for heterosexual relations is 16.[1]
* Sexual activity among youth is taking place at much younger ages than was true 10-20 years ago.[2]

Contraception

* Sterilization has become one of the most common forms of birth control for married men and women over the age of thirty.[3]
* Approximately 10,000 men and women are sterilized each year.[3]
* The overall use of condoms in Norway suggests that they are used more for birth control than a means to protect against sexually transmitted disease.[3]
* 71% of women use some form of contraception.[4]

Abortion[5]

* In January of 1979, a law was passed to make abortion legal up to twelve weeks gestation.
* After twelve weeks, a board of doctors makes the decision whether or not to abort the fetus.
* The legalization of abortion did not increase the rate of abortions from 1974 to 1984. After 1985, the abortion rate did increase somewhat.
* Illegal abortions are rare in Norway, but if a woman has been refused a second trimester abortion, she may travel to another country to have one.

Sex Education

* No information available.

STD's including AIDS[6]

* As of 9/30/95, there were 482 cases of AIDS diagnosed.
* It is estimated that 1,250 people are living with HIV in Norway.

Homosexuality

* Homosexuality is accepted in Norway; same-sex partnerships are recognized.[7]
* Age of consent for homosexual and lesbian relations is 16.[1]
* There is no discrimination of homosexuals in the military.[1]
* Laws prohibiting discrimination on the grounds of sexual orientation were introduced in 1981.[8]
* Foreign partners of lesbian women and gay men can be granted residence rights on proof of a long-term relationship.[8]

Prostitution[9]

* Prostitution is legal in Norway.
* There are some laws prohibiting prostitution in public places.
* Pimping is illegal.
* Age of consent is 16.
* The main forms of prostitution are street prostitution and private advertising for sexual services.

Pornography

* No information is available.

Resources

Norwegian Association for Sexual and Reproductive Health (NSSR), Landskronaveien 179, 2013 Skjetten, Norway. Tel: (47) 6384 0276.

References

1. Alan F. Reekie, "Age of Consent Laws in the Council of Europe States in 1993," <http://ftp.tcp.com/qrd/world/europe/age.of.consent.laws-12.20.94>.

2. G. Kelly, Sexuality Today (Guildford, CT: Brown & Benchmark, 1995), p. 162.

3. K. Mahler, "Condom use increase in Norway appears related more to contraception than to disease prevention," Family Planning Perspectives, Mar.-Apr. (1996).

4. The Economist Book of World Vital Statistics. (1990). Times Books.

5. H. Skjelle, International Handbook on Abortion, (Westport: CT, 1988).

6. World Health Organization: The Current Global Situation of the HIV/AIDS Pandemic. Dec. (1995).

7. http://www.qrd.org/qrd/world/europe/norway.

8. P. Snyder, The European Women's Almanac, New York, NY: Columbia University Proess, 1992), p. 262.

9. The World Sex Guide. Last Updated: 1996/04/30. (C) 1994, 1995, 1996 Atta and M. <an48932@anon.penet.fi>.

POLAND
POPULATION: 38.5 MILLION

Capital:
W a r s a w
(population: 1,651,200)

Major Cities & Populations: Warsaw: 1,651,200;   Krakow: 744,000

Ethnic Groups: Polish 98%; German 1%; Ukrainian 0.6%; Byelorussian 0.5%

Languages: Polish

Major Religions: Roman Catholic 95%; Eastern Orthodox, Protestant, and other 5%

Annual Income per Person: $4,900

Urban Population: 61%.

Infant Mortality: 13 per 1000 births

Life Expectancy: Females: 77 years; Males: 69 years

Adult Literacy: 98%

Health Care System: Hospitals, Private Physicians

References:
"Poland" The CIA Factbook,   http://www.odcl.gov/cia/publications/95fact/ch.html
(retrieved June 10, 1996)
1993 Grolier Electronic Publishing, Inc.
1992 Population Reference Bureau, Inc.

Sexual   Activity

* Legal age of consent for sex: Male-Female: 15,   Male-Male: 15,   Female-Female: 15.[1]

Contraception[2]

* Contraception use is low due to the lack of availability.
* 80% of women respondents claim that they use contraception; the methods chosen are withdrawal or rhythm rather than the Pill or IUD.
* Heavy church influences have caused pharmacists to give up stocking effective contraceptives.

Abortion

* Abortions are legal in Poland for the following reasons: 1) The pregnancy endangers the life or is a serious risk to the health of the mother; 2) Prenatal diagnosis confirms there is serious and irreversible damage to the fetus; or 3) The pregnancy has resulted from a criminal act such as rape or incest.[2]
* The suspected high incidence of abortion is due to several factors, including shortage of low-cost, high-quality modern contraceptives and less reliable natural methods of fertility control and a lack of comprehensive sex education programs.[3]

Sex   Education[4]

* Sex education in Poland has been compulsory since 1972.
* In 1994 a new law obligated the government to provide sexuality education in schools.
* A book completed by the Board of Education: <u>Preparing for Family Life</u>, has met with opposition from sex educators due to its content supporting the church's view on abortion and contraception use.

STD's, including AIDS

* Hepatitis B: 34 notified cases per 100,000.[5]
* 10,000 cases of AIDS, 50% of adult prevalence rate.[6]

Homosexuality[7]

* Sexual orientation (gay rights) has been added to Poland's constitution, in the section on protection from discrimination.

Prostitution[8]

* Prostitution is completely unregulated, and legal.

Pornography[9]

* Illegal, although posters and calendars of naked women are available.
* Pornographic films are distributed by video clubs.
* Female bodies (half or full nudes) are used to advertise many goods.

Resources

*Polish Sexoloigical Society, ul. Londynska 12m 31, 03-921 Warsawa, Poland.

References

1. PinkBoard HomePage: "Legal Age of Consent"
<http://www.pinkboard.com.au/consent.html>

2. B. Rolston, A. Eggert, (editors). <u>Abortion in the New Europe: A Comparative Handbook,</u> (Westport, CT: 1994) p. xxvi.

3. United Nations, <u>Abortion Policies: A Global Review, Vol.III.</u> 1995, p. 37-39.

4. G. Mrugala, "Polish Family Planning in Crisis: The Roman Catholic Influence" <u>Planned Parenthood in Europe</u> (1991), Vol. 20, No. 2, p. 5

5. Linglof TO, "Hepatitis B in parts of former USSR." <u>HealthGate Data Corp</u>. MedGate Access Plan, updated June 25, 1996.

6. <u>World Health Organization, Global programme on AIDS</u>, December 1995, <http://gpawww.who.ch/aidscase/dec1995/hivtext.html>

7. B. Skolander, "Poland's Draft Constitution Includes Sexual Orientation" <u>GayLinc</u>,Jan. 11, 1996 <http://www.dds.nl/gaylinc/poland1.html>

8. <u>World Sex Guide</u>, Prostitution in Poland: last update: 1996. <http://www.paranoia.com/faq/prostitution/Netherlands.html>

9. E. Zielinska & J. Plakwicz, "Strengthening Human Rights for Women and Men in Matters Relating to Sexual Behaviors and Reproduction," <u>Journal of Women's History,</u> (1994),vol. 5(3), p. 91.

PORTUGAL
POPULATION: 10.5 MILLION

Capital:
Lisbon
(population: 1,612,000)

Major Cities & Populations: Lisbon 1,612,000; Oporto 1,315,000

Ethnic Groups: Portuguese 99%; Cape Verdean, Brazilian, Spanish, and British

Languages: Portuguese (official)

Major Religions: Roman Catholic 97%

Annual Income per Person: $5,620

Urban Population: 34%

Infant Mortality: 9 per 1,000 live births

Life Expectancy: Females 78 years; Males 71 years

Adult Literacy: 87%

Health Care System: National Health Services and Private hospitals; 1 doctor per 344 people.

References:
Encyclopedic World Atlas (1994) NY: Oxford University Press
The World Almanac and Book of Facts 1996 (1995) Mahwah, NJ: World Almanac Books
Country report of Portugal a general overview of prostitution in Portugal,
http://allserv.reg.ac.be/~rmak/europap/rappor.html, 6/14/96.

Sexual Activity

* Age of consent for heterosexual intercourse is 16 in Portugal.[1]

Contraception[2]

* Safe contraception is not widespread.
* Oral Contraceptives (The Pill) sold in pharmacies without medical prescription.
* In 1980 withdrawal was the most popular method of birth control.

Abortion

* Abortion is legal only under certain circumstances, up to 12 weeks:[3]
  -Risk to life of woman
  -Risk to woman's physical health or mental health
  -Rape or other sexual crimes
  -Unborn child will suffer without possible cure from serious disease or malformation (up to 16 weeks)
* The majority of abortions are done for economic reasons, many without husband's knowledge.[2]
* Two medical opinions are required before an abortion will be performed.[2]
* All requests for abortion are evaluated by ethical or technical commissions.[2]
* Abortion remains an uneasy subject for health professionals, it is a subject they prefer to ignore.[2]
* Abortions are performed free of charge.[3]
* Majority of abortions are still performed illegally by doctors, nurses, midwives and private clinics.[2]

Sex Education

* The Law of 1984, gave the right to sex education and family planning[2] into the school curriculum.[4]
* Without the implementation of law there exists no sex education component in the curriculum.[4]

STDs, including AIDS

* 3,344 AIDS cases reported as of 6/19/96.[5]
* AIDS is not seen as a gay disease, due to intelligent information campaigns.[6]
* There is no epidemiological surveillance of STDs, most patients are not examined by health care professional but treat themselves with antibiotics easily obtained over the counter.[7]

Homosexuality

* Article 71 of the Penal Code which ban's "acts against nature" has been used against lesbian women and gay men. Other legislation has been used to deny lesbian and gay parents custody of thier children after divorce.[8]
* Homosexuality is "not" illegal in Portugal, since everyone in entitled to choose his/her own destiny.[9]
* Age of consent for lesbian or gay sex is 16 years old.[1]
* ILGA - PORTUGAL (International Lesbian and Gay Association) is Portugal's only gay organization.[9]
* The concept of homosexuality as an illness was dropped from scientific writings in 1979.[6]
* Gays and Lesbians are afraid to come out because of lack of support from family or groups.[9]

Prostitution[7]

* Prostitution was legal in Portugal until 12/31/94.
* Opinion towards prostitution is ambiguous, different attitudes towards female, male and child varies greatly. Female prostitution is tolerated while male and child prostitution is not accepted and is much more hidden.

Pornography[10]

* The legal age for viewing pornography in Portugal is 18.

Resources

*Associacao Para o Planeamento da Familia (APF), 38 Rua Artilharia um 2DT, 1200 Lisbon, Portugal. Tel: (351 1) 385 3993; Fax: (351 1) 388 7379.

References

1. Age-of-consent laws of the world, http://www.c2.org/~prd/world/acc.htlm. 06/19/96.

2. B. Ralson and A. Eggert, Abortion in the New Europe: A Comparative handbook, (Westport, CT: Greenwood Press, 1994), pp. 215-227.

3. National Abortion Campaign, Abortion Laws in Europe (London, England, 1995).

4. P. Meredith and L. Thomas, Planned Parenthood in Europe: A Human Rights Perspective (London: International Planned Parenthood, 1986).

5. European information center for HIV and AIDS, http://www.hiv.net, 06/19/96.

6. W. Dynes, Encyclopedia of Homosexuality Vol. 2 M-index, (NY: Garland Publishing Inc., 1990), pp. 1329-30.

7. Country report of Portugal general overview of prostitution in Portugal, http://allserv.rug.ac.be/~rmak/europap/rappor.html,   06/14/96.

8. P. Snyder, The European Woman's Almanac (New York, NY: Columbia University Press, 1992), p. 291.

9. Gay life in Portugal, http://www5.servtech.com/ilga/life.html,   06/14/96.

10. Restricted access: Legal age for viewing pornography, http://www.pinkboard.com.au:80/r.html,   06/18/96.

ROMANIA
POPULATION: 23 MILLION

Capital:
Bucharest
(population: 2 million)

Major Cities & Populations: Bucharest: 2 million; Constana: 350,000

Ethnic Groups: Romanian 89%; Hungarian 9%; German 0.4%; Ukrainian, Serb, Croat, Russian Turk, and Gypsy 2%

Languages: Romanian, Hungarian, German

Major Religions: Romanian Orthodox 70%, Roman Catholic 6%, Protestant 6%, Unaffiliated 18%

Annual Income per Person: $2,700

Urban Population: 53%

Infant Mortality: 19 per 1000 births

Life Expectancy: Females: 75 yrs. Males: 69 yrs.

Adult Literacy: 97%

Health Care System: Hospitals, Private Physicians

References:
"Romania" The CIA Factbook, http://www.odcl.gov/cia/publications/95fact/ch.html (retrieved June 10, 1996)
1993 Grolier Electronic Publishing, Inc.
1992 Population Reference Bureau, Inc

Sexual Activity

* No information available.

Contraception[1]

* Modern contraceptives are only sporadically available at a cost similar to abortion.
* Reproductive services are mostly controlled by underpaid state-employed gynecologists.
* Due to the lack of modern contraceptives, fears of their side-effects and limited access to family planning services, women tend to rely on natural methods of birth control and abortion.
* Percentage of types of contraception used: Withdrawal: 25%, Rhythm: 6%; Condom: 3%; IUD: 3%,; Pill: 2%; Tubal Ligation: 1%; Spermicides: 0.5%; No Method: 59%.

Abortion[2]

* As of 1989 the new government of Romania abolished the law that prohibited abortions. This led to a surge in legally performed abortions from 109,819 in 1989 to 913,973 in 1990.
* In 1991 the rate abortions women were having was three abortions to every one birth
* Many Romanian women accept abortions as a primary form of contraception due to their misconceptions about other forms of birth control.

Sex Education[3]

* Sex education was removed from the school system in the early 1980's.
* Few efforts to introduce sex and contraception education into the secondary schools have been met with opposition from teachers and parents.
* The major sources of contraception and sex information: Friend (45%), Mass media (19%), Health care providers (10%).

STD's, including AIDS[4]

* 500 cases of AIDS; .004% of adult prevalence rate.

Homosexuality[5]

* Homosexuality is legal except in cases where it causes a "public scandal," involves a minor, a defenceless person, or if it is by coercion or rape; jail terms of up to five years in prison.
* Homosexual propaganda and proselytism are banned.

Prostitution[6]

* Child prostitution is a problem due to the large number of unwanted children. Under dictator Nicolae Ceausescu, abortion was illegal, contraceptives unavailable and sex education non-existent.
* More recently, the Romanian government has agreed to pay for 15 workers to maintain contact with street children and run a community center with medical services for them.

Pornography

* No information available.

Resources

Society for Education in Contraception & Sexuality (SECS), Calea 13 Septembrie nr. 85 BI.77C, sc. 1, et.8, ap.75, sector 5, Bucharest, Romania. Tel: (40 1) 781 6661; Fax: (40 1) 410 1097.

References

1. B. Johnson, M. Horga, & L. Andronache, "Contraception and Abortion in Romania." The Lancet (April 3, 1993) Vol. 341, p. 875-878.

2. F. Serbanescu, L. Morris, & A. Stanescu, "The Impact of Recent Policy Changes on Fertility, Abortion, and Contraception Use in Romania." Studies in Family Planning (March/April 1995), Vol. 26, No. 2, p. 81.

3. F. Serbanescu, L. Morris, & A. Stanescu, "The Impact of Recent Policy Changes on Fertility, Abortion, and Contraception Use in Romania." Studies in Family Planning (March/April 1995), Vol. 26, No. 2, p. 84.

4. World Health Organization, Global programme on AIDS, December 1995, <http://gpawww.who.ch/aidscase/dec1995/hivtext.html>

5. R. Buckmire: "Romanian Senate Amends Homosexual Ban," Feb 5, 1994, <buckmr@rpi.edu>

6. P. Knox, "Youth-Sex Trade Flourishes in Post-Communist Eastern Europe." <http://www.paranoia.com> (retrieved 1/6/97).

RUSSIA
POPULATION: 147.5 MILLION

Capital:
Moscow
(population: 9 Million)

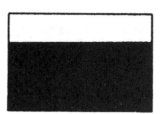

Major Cities & Populations: Moscow 9 million; St. Petersburg 4.4 million; Nizhniy Novgorod 1.4 million; Novosibirsk 1.4 million

Ethnic Groups: Russian 83%; Tatar 4%; Ukrainian 3%; Chuvash 2%; over 100 others

Languages: Russian 87%; Ukrainian, Uzbek, Armenian, Azerbaijani, Georgian, Belarussian, many others

Major Religions: Russian Orthodox 25%; nonreligious 60%

Annual Income per Person: $4,820

Urban Population: 73%

Infant Mortality: 13 per 1,000 births

Life Expectancy: Females: 74 years; Males: 64 years

Adult Literacy: 98%

Health Care System: 1 doctor per 226 people; 1 bed per 74

References:
Encyclopedic World Atlas (1994) NY: Oxford University Press.
The World Almanac and Book of Facts (1995) Mahwah, NJ: World Almanac Books
"Russia" The CIA Factbook, http://www.odcl.gov/cia/publications/95fact/ch.html
(retrieved June 10, 1996)

Sexual Activity

* Premarital sexual relations in Russia are more widespread than ever before, indicating that the age at which people are having sexual intercourse has decreased.[1]
* The average age of first intercourse for girls is now 16.[2]
* Sexual activity before marriage is typical for the majority of today's youth: 79% of young married women and 75% of young married men had sexual intercourse before marriage.[1]

Contraception

* Abortion has been the main method of birth control, because of the lack of choice.[3]
* Use of contraceptives is low: A 1990 survey found that only 22% of women are regular contraceptive users.[4]
* Modern contraceptives like the IUD and Pill are used by few women due to lack of availability and negative attitudes.[5]
* Emergency Contraception is available: Postinor is packaged in a 4-pill strip with directions for women to take one tablet immediately after intercourse, but to use no more than four tablets per month.[6]

Abortion

* Russia was the world's first country to legalize abortion. In 1920 the Communist Party legalized abortion in an attempt to destroy the traditional family and religion, and to create a new social basis for Russian Communist society. However, in 1936 the law was repealed and abortion was illegal. Abortion became legal again in 1955.[4]
* On average every woman born in Russia has four or five abortions.[7]
* In 1993, 3.2 million induced abortions were officially registered.[1]
* Illegal abortion is common (the number of illegl abortions is thought to equal the number of legal abortions).[4]
* The widespread use of abortion has been found to be accompanied by harmful side effects and problems in future pregnancies; one of the most common causes of infertility is scarring from abortion.[8]

146

Sex Education

* Sex education does not exist in the school curricula; the Family Planning Association is the main agency involved in sex education.[9]
* A recent study found that the majority of Russians are supportive of sexuality education in schools.[1]
* There is increased interest in developing sexuality education programs. For example, in 1995, the Ministry of Education announced a competition for organizations to develop a sexuality program for high schools.[10]

STDS, including AIDS

* There has been a rapid surge in syphilis and gonorrhea cases in parts of the former USSR (Estonia, Lithuania, Lativa and Russia).[11]
* There is an frightening increase among young people of venereal disease and AIDS. Every fifth case of syphilis diagnosed is recorded in a teenager under 17 years of age and a third of new occurrences of gonorrhea are in teenagers under 17.[12]
* The first AIDS case was reported in 1987; as of 1994, 717 people had tested HIV positive and 83 people had died.[13]
* Russia has a mandatory HIV testing for foreigners.[14]

Homosexuality

* In 1993 the Russian Parliment enacted a new penal code which no longer includes the prohibition of homosexuality.[15]
* Negative attitudes about homosexuality persist: A 1994 poll found that 23 percent of Russians believed that homosexuals should be executed, 32 percent said they should be isolated; only 12 percent said they should be left in peace.[16]

Prostitution

* In 1987, the Supreme Soviet of the Russian Republic made prostitution an administrative offense punishable by fines up to 200 rubles ($360).[17]
* The Soviet attempt to eradicate prostitution in the 1920s (by encouraging female employment, job-training, and government clinics & housing) is still considered more progressive than the alternatives used in countries around the world today of regulation, prosecution, or decriminalization.[18]

147

Pornography

* The collapse of communism in the former USSR has brought about a resurgance of commercially available sexually explicit materials. The problem became so acute that Prime Minister Mikhail Gorbachev had to appoint a committee to suggest measures to safeguard Russian morality.[19]
* The criminal code in Russia outlaws the sale of pornography, but does not clearly define what exactly pornography is.[20]
* Moscow authorities banned the sale of highly profitable erotic material on the Russian capital's streets and in transit stations. To protect children from pornography, which was rare in the former Soviet Union until the mid 1980s, the city council restricted sales of adult publications to designated shops and ordered sexually explicit materials wrapped in plastic to prevent perusal by minors. It also made illegal the sale of pornography to and by anyone under 16.[21]
* Television shows do not cut to commercials as the show gets "steamy" - they often follow the naked couple to bed.[20]

Resources

*Center for Formation of Sexual Culture, ul. Pionerskaya, 19 Mediko-Padagogicheskaya Shkola, Yoroslavl 150044.
*Russian Family Planning Association, 18/20 Vadkovsky per., 101479 Moscow
*Russian Sexological Association, Krylatskiye Kholmy, 30-2, 207 Moscow.

References

1. V. Bodravo, "Russian Attitudes on Sex and Youth," Choices (1996), 25(1), p. 9-14.
2. I. Alesina, "Adolescent Sexual Health Initiative in Russia," Choices (1996), 25(2), p. 16-17.
3. A. Visser et al, "Contraception in Russia: Attitude, Knowledge and Practice of Doctors," Planned Parenthood in Europe (1993), 22(2), p. 26-29.
4. A. Popov, "A Short History of Abortion and Population Policy in Russia," Planned Parenthood in Europe (1993), 22(2), p. 23-25.
5. P. Lehert et al, "Contraception in the Former USSR: Recent Survey Results on Women's Behavior and Attitudes," Planned Parenthood in Europe (1992), 21, p. 9-11.
6. C. Ellertson et al "Expanding Access to Emergency Contraception in Developing Countries," Studies in Family Planning (1995), 26(5), p. 251-263.
7. I. Grebesheva, "Abortion and the Problems of Family Planning in Russia," Planned Parenthood in Europe (1992), 21(2), p. 8.
8. A. Khomassuridze, "Abortion and Contraception in the USSR," Progress Postponed: Abortion in Europe in the 1990s (London: IPPF, 1993), p. 78-91.
9. D. Vilar, "School Sex Education: Still a Priority in Europe," Planned Parenthood in Europe (1994), 23(3), p. 8-12.
10. V. Popova, "Sexuality Education Moves Forward in Russia," SIECUS Report (NY: SIECUS, 1996), 24(3), p. 14-15.
11. T. Linglof, "Rapid Increase of Syphilis and Gonorrhea in Parts of the Former USSR," Sexually Transmitted Diseases (1995), 22(3), p. 160.
12. I. Grebesheva, "Abortion and the Problems of Family Planning in Russia," Planned Parenthood in Europe (1992), 21(2), p. 8.
13. S. Efron, Russia's Epidemic of Shame," Los Angeles Times (April 5, 1994), p. A1.
14. "Russia Oks AIDS Tests for Foreigners," Contemporay Sexuality (published by AASECT, December, 1994) 28(12), p. 14.
15. "Comparative Survey of the Legal and Societal Situation of Homosexuals in Europe," http://www.quality.org/FQRD/assocs/ilga/euroletter/35-survey.html (retrieved 6/24/96)
16. "Gay Russians Remain In," Contemporay Sexuality (published by AASECT, August, 1995) 29(8), p. 9.
17. L. Anthony, "Sex and the Soviet Man," National Review (July 8, 1988), p. 24-25.
18.J. Quigley, "The Dilemma of Prostitution Law Reform," American Criminal Law Review (1992), 29(4), p. 1192-1234.
19. H. Goscilo, "New Members and Organs: Politics of Porn," Genders (1995), 22, p. 164.
20. G. Kelly, Sexuality Today, (Guilford, CT: Brown & Benchmark, 1995), p. 434.
21. R. Holman, "Moscow Restricts Pornography," Wall Street Journal (6/6/94), p. A9.

SINGAPORE
POPULATION: 2.9 MILLION

Capital:
Singapore
(population: 2.7 million)

Major Cities and Populations	Singapore 2.7 million
Ethnic Groups:	Chinese 77%, Malay 15%, Indian 6%
Languages:	Chinese, Malay, Tamil, English (all official)
Major Religions:	Buddhist 29%, Christian 19%, Muslin 16%, Taoist 13%
Income Per Capita:	$15,000
Urban Population:	100%
Infant Mortality:	6 per 1000 live births
Life Expectancy:	Female 79 years, male 73 years
Adult Literacy:	91%
Health Care System:	One of the highest health standards in Southeast Asia.

References:
Worldmark Encyclopedia or the Nations: Asia and Oceania, Vol. 4, Eighth Edition, pp. 443-454, Gale Research Inc., Detroit, 1995.
The World Almanac and Book of Facts 1996 (1995), Mahwah, NJ: World Almanac Books

Sexual   Activity

* In the early 1970's, Singapore attempted to reduce its population through national programs, including financial incentive for sterilization. By 1984, this was working too well, and by 1987, the birth shortfall was judged to be detrimental to the country. Sterilization incentives were no longer available to better educated families, although it was retained for less-educated families, as well as those with three or more children. Three children was seen as the optimal family size. Advertising reflected this view.[1]
* Lee Kuan Yew, Singapore's founding leader suggested that polygamy may be a solution to one of Singapore's major problems: better educated women are less likely to marry and procreate, leaving the less educated women to have the majority of Singapore's offspring.[2]

Contraception[3]

* Poorly educated families are offered approximately $500 per year for 20 years plus educational aid for their children to parents participating in a family planning program. These parents must also agree to have no more than two children. If a third child is born, or if the parents divorce, the payments stop.

Abortion

* Abortion ends about one third of all pregnancies in Singapore.[4]
* Ninety-five percent of all abortions are performed before the 13th week of pregnancy.[5]
* Seventy-two percent of all abortions are performed on married women.[5]
* Abortion was legalized in 1970, and was completely liberalized in 1975. This has led to the abolition of criminal abortions, allowing any woman access to a safer procedure.[5]

Sex   Education[2]

* It has been noted that Singaporean women are highly ignorant of their bodies, including not being able to locate their vaginas. Women complain also of pain during intercourse, due to the lack of foreplay. Others believe that they are barren, but who actually turn out to be virgins, according to prominent gynecologist Vytialingam Atputharajah.

STDs, including AIDS

* The Department of STD Control, in Singapore provides medical education about STDs and AIDS, as well as safer sex. Campaigns include condom advertisements.[6]
* One hundred eleven new cases of HIV were reported in 1995, an increase of 29%.[7]
* 419 HIV cases have been reported as of February of 1996.[7]
* 179 people to date have been reported as having AIDS, and 124 have died.[7]
* 91% of HIV infected people are men, and 76% of the transmissions occurred through heterosexual contact.[7]

Homosexuality

* Homosexuality is outlawed in Singapore.[2]
* In recent censorship legislation, homosexual images were banned from the Internet, due to being known as "sexual perversions."[8]

Prostitution[9]

* Prostitution is legal, but operating a brothel and public soliciting are not. In Designated Red-light Areas (DRAs), it is officially tolerated.
* Age of consent for prostitutes is 16.
* Working women must carry a yellow card stating that they are registered and have recently had a health exam.
* Some brothels provide benefits to keep employees.
* Prostitutes do not work because of financial necessity, since there is no poverty and nearly full employment in Singapore.

Pornography

* In Singapore, the Internet is regulated as though it were a broadcast medium. Political and religious content providers must register with the state.[10]
* Sexually explicit material has been censored by the Ministry of Information and the Arts.[10]
* Only recently was a ban on R-rated movies lifted, by former Prime Minister Goh Chok Tong.[11]
* Recent new laws prohibit pornography, including "sexual perversions" such as homosexuality on the Internet.[12]
* A Government-appointed panel determines what is banned from books, magazines, public, films, newspapers, etc. in Singapore.[12]

Resources

*Singapore Planned Parenthood Association, 03-04 Pek Chuan Bldg., 116 Lavender St., Singapore, 1233.

References

1. Jonah M. David, "Don't Count on Me, Singapore," National Review, Vol. 46, No. 9, May 16, 1994.

2. John Chua, "Unstudly," The New Republic, vol. 206, No. 4, Jan 27, 1992, pp. 11-12.

3. The Wall Street Journal, Aug. 16, 1993, p. A10, col. 4.

4. "Birth of Another Nation," The Economist, Vol 314, No. 7645, Mar. 10, 1990, p. 37.

5. Paul Sachdev, International Handbook on Abortion, Greenwood Press, Inc., Westport, CT, 1988, pp. 402-412.

6. "Department of STD Control," <http://biomed.nus.sg/dsc/dsc.html>, last updated 8/16/95.

7. "AIDS Daily Summary," <http://abacus.oxy.edu/qrd/aids/cdc/daily.summaries/>, 2/22/96.

8. David B. Allan, "Gay Law News," GayLawNet, <http://www.labyrinth.net.au/`dba>, last updated 8/24/96.

9. The World Sex Guide, "Prostitution in: Singapore," <http://www.paranoia.com/faq/prostitution/Singapore.html> last updated 4/30/96.

10. "Human Rights Watch Silencing the Net: The Threat to Freedom of Expression On-line," <http://www.epic.org/free_speech/hrw_report_5_96.html> 5/96.

11. Philip Shenon, "Back to Somerset Maugham and Life's Seamy Side," The New York Times, Vol 141, p. A4, Col 2, Oct. 10, 1991.

12. David B. Allan, "Gay Law News," GayLawNet, <http://www.labyrinth.net.au/`dba>, last updated 8/24/96.

SLOVAKIA
POPULATION: 5.4 MILLION

Capital:
Bratislava
(population: 442,000)

Major   Cities   and   Populations Kosice 235,000

Ethnic   Groups: 85% Slovak, 11.5% Hungarian, Romany,
                                  Ruthenians, Czechs

Languages: Slovak (official), Hungarian

Major   Religions: Roman Catholic 74%, Protestant

Income   Per   Capita: $5,800

Urban   Population: 57%

Infant   Mortality: 10 per 1000 births

Life   Expectancy: Female 78 years, MaleS 69 years

Adult   Literacy: 99%

Health   Care   System: State health insurance, high
                                  immunization rates

References:
Worldmark Encyclopedia of the Nations: Europe, Vol. 5, Eighth Edition, pp. 383-390,
Gale Research Inc, Detroit, 1995.
The World Almanac and Book of Facts 1996 (1995), Mahwah, NJ: World Almanac Book.
"Slovakia" The CIA Factbook,   http://www.odcl.gov/cia/publications/95fact/ch.html
(retrieved June 10, 1996)

Sexual Activity

* Age of consent for sexual activity is 15.[1]

Contraception

* Due to the lack of use of reliable contraception methods, abortion has been the most reliable family planning practice.[2]
* Only 28% of women at risk for unplanned pregnancy use modern contraceptives.[2]
* Gynecologists view condoms as somewhat convenient, and only somewhat reliable against pregnancy and disease.[2]
* Only 65% of gynecologists think that abstinence is 100% reliable against unplanned pregnancy and sexually transmitted disease, and only 39% of them perceived this as a 'very safe' method. Five percent viewed it as a convenient method.[2]
* Eighty percent of gynecologists prescribe the Pill very often, and 63% of them view it as 100% reliable, while only 25% of them perceive it to be 'very safe.' Ninety percent believe that the Pill is very convenient.[2]
* There is a relatively restrictive law on voluntary sterilization.[3]
* Only 6% of at-risk women were using hormonal contraception, 13% used IUDs, and 5% had been sterilized, according to the first national contraceptive prevalence survey.[3]
* The Slovak Family Planning Association is attempting to improve the public's knowledge about contraception, and to change negative attitudes.[3]
* The Slovak Family Planning Association is also attempting to introduce legislation on voluntary sterilization.[3]
* Postinor, an emergency contraceptive from Hungary, is registered in Slovakia.[4]

Abortion

* Abortion available on request up to 12 weeks.[5]
* Available in the second trimester for medical reasons, risk .to the mother or the fetus, or for rape and other sexual crimes.[5]
* There must be at least 6 months between abortions, with the exception of women with at least two births, aged 35 or more, or in the case of rape.[5]
* Recommendation of physician is needed.[5]
* Parental consent for minors under the age of 16.[5]

* For women aged 16-18, parents must be informed by physician after abortion.[5]
* Counselling is required.[5]
* In a 1992 survey of 6,000 women, 74% answered "Yes" to the following question: "Do you think that women should decide themselves about the birth of a child if they have a broad understanding of this topic based on thorough education and professional advice in this field?"[3]

Sex   Education

* Some sex education subjects exist in school curricula, under the title of Family Life Education.[6]
* Family Planning Association considers these programs to be conservative.[6]
* Family Planning Association is the main agency involved in sex education.[6]
* Sex education activities include lectures to parents and youth.[6]
* Family Planning Association provides educational materials.[6]
* Slovakia's high abortion rate is attributed, in part, to inadequacies in school sex education.[3]
* Slovakia's Family Planning Association is working to influence public opinion about such topics through the use of mass media, and they are trying to create a comprehensive planned parenthood network.[3]
* Collection of statistical data must be completed.[3]
* The Slovak Family Planning Association and the Slovak Woman's Social Democracy Community are working to form a sex education curriculum for school children.[3]
* Problems with such programs include a lack of available resources published in Slovak, moral support, lack of international standards and human rights education.[3]

STDs,   including   AIDS[7]

* As of December 1991, there were only 30 HIV positive individuals in the Slovak Republic.
* There has been national infection surveillance in effect, so underreporting is unlikely.
* The blood supply has been screened since 1986.
* The low prevalence for HIV infection is likely due to political isolation.
* Sexual contact seems to be the primary mode of HIV transmission, but homosexual promiscuity appears to be low.

Homosexuality

* Age of consent for homosexuals and lesbians is 15.[1]
* Homosexual promiscuity appears to be limited.[7]
* Recently, a lesbian group was formed in Bratislava.[8]

Prostitution[9]

* Prostitution is larger and more organized than it was in 1989, at the end of Soviet rule.
* Recently, entrepreneurs have opened massage parlors in Slovakia. Prostitutes generally have 'bodyguards' to bring them to and from clients.
* Inconsistent legislation allows the use of legal business premises for sexual services.
* The general feeling about prostitution is negative, and this attitude shows in a quote by Slovakian Interior Ministry member Tibor Shellberger: "We can say that prostitution today has become a very advantageous branch of international organized crime."

Pornography[10]

* In 1995, Slovakia began allowing private television on VTV Cable. The Company will not broadcast programs with erotic scenes, pronography, violence and brutality.

Resources

*Slovak Association for Family Planning and Parenthood Education, Ruzinovska 1, 821 02 Bratislava.

References

1. Alan F. Reekie, "Age of Consent Laws int he Council of Europe States in 1993," <http://ftp.tcp.com/qrd/world/europe/age.of.consent.laws-12.20.94>.

2. Adriaan Visser, Radim Uzel, Every Ketting, Nico Bruyniks, Bjoern Oddens, "Practice, Attitudes and Knowledge of Czech and Slovak Gynaecologists Concerning Contraception, " <u>Planned Parenthood in Europe</u>, Vol. 23, No. 1, 1994.

3. Alena Chudikova, "Reproductive Health Challenges in the Slovak Republic," <u>Planned Parenthood in Europe</u>, Vol. 22, No. 3, p. 27, 1993.

4. Sharon Camp, "Postinor--the Unique Method of Emergency Contraception Developed in Hungary, " <u>Planned Parenthood in Europe</u>, Vol. 24, No. 2, August, pp. 23-24, 1995.

5. Abortion Laws in Europe (amended Jan 1995)

6. Duarte Vilar, "School Sex Education: Still a Priority in Europe," <u>Planned Parenthood in Europe</u>, Vol. 23, No. 3, pp 8-12 (1994).

7. Vlastimil Mayer, Gail Shor-Posner, Marianna K. Baum, "Czech and Slovak Federal Republic: Not Too Late to Slow HIV-1 Spread," <u>The Lancet</u>, Vol. 339, No. 8802, May 9, 1992, p. 1162.

8. Rex Wockner, "International News #21 (September 22, 1994)," <http://www.casti.com/AusQRD/world/1994/wockner-21.html>, 8/27/96.

9. Slavka Blazsekova, "Highway to Prostitution," <http://www.jmk.su.se/jmk/eurorep/21.html>, 8/27/96.

10. SDS Media Digest, "VTV: Dawn of Private Slovak TV?" <http://www.eunet.sk/media/95/Apr/0023.html>, 8/27/96.

SOUTH AFRICA
POPULATION: 45 MILLION

Capital:
Pretoria
(population: 823,000)

Major Cities & Population:	Cape Town 2.4 million; Durban 1.1 million; Johannesburg 1.9 million
Ethnic Groups:	Black 75%; White 14%; Coloured 9%; Indian 3%; Galician 7%; Basque 2%
Languages:	11 official languages incuding: English, Afrikaans, Ndebele
Major Religions:	Mainly Christian 31%; Dutch Reform 23%; Roman Catholic 15%; Hindu 3%
Annual Income per Person:	$2,530
Urban Population:	63%
Infant Mortality:	46 per 1,000
Life Expectancy:	Females 68 years; Males 63 years
Adult Literacy:	76% (Whites 98%; Blacks 32%)
Health Care System:	Private clinics, gov't supported programs; 1 doctor per 1,264 people.

References:
Encyclopedic World Atlas (1994) NY: Oxford University Press.
The World Almanac and Book of Facts 1996 (1995) Mahwah, NJ: World Almanac Books.

Sexual   Activity

* The typical age of first intercourse: 16 years old.[1]
* Polygyny (multiple wives) is practiced by 15-30% of married men.[1]
* The Contraceptive Prevalence Survey found that 1 woman out of 7 women had their first pregnancy while in school.[1]
* Sexual activity is more in the open now that apartheid is abolished.[2]

Contraception

* In 1932, the government founded the Family Planning Association; it has 5,000 moblie sites that provide people with information and contraceptives.[3]
* The most common methods of contraception by race are: Whites: Pill (21%); Blacks: Injection (26%); Colored: Injection (27%); Indian: Sterilization (25%).[3]
* Family Planning services are free of charge to all races.[3]
* Emergency Contraception is not widely used; it is only given to 100 patients annually.[4]

Abortion

* Abortion is illegal unless it's done by a medical practitioner in a state hospital under the following conditions: 1) when the pregnancy endangers a women's life, 2) if she's raped, or 3) the child could be born with a serious birth defect.[5]
* In order for an abortion to be obtained, one medical practitioner must be a psychiatrist who can certify that pregnancy will damage the women's health.[5]
* 800-1,000 legal abortions are performed each year. Of these, 77% of them are performed for psychiatric reasons.[6]
* There is an estimate 200,000 illegal abortion a year.[5]
* Blacks make up 60% of the illegal abortion rate.[5]
* The Abortion Reform Action Group campaigns for a humane law "for the right of every woman and every race to terminate undesired pregnancy." Other groups include: The National Council of Women, and the Women's Bureau. These groups are working to change the abortion law.[5]

Sex Education

* The Population Development Program educates people about contraception.[3]
* According to the African National Congress Policy Guidelines for a Democratic South Africa, sex education and family planning will be included as part of a future national health program.[3]
* Since a new constitution has been made which protects free speech, sex in magazines and films is legal. Sex education will be required in schools in the near future.[2]

STDs, including AIDS

* The number of AIDS cases as of Decemeber 1993 is 3,458.[7]
* The number of AIDS cases has increased 10 fold since 1990; by the year 2000 health officals predict there will be 8 million cases.[8]
* HIV infection rates in newborns is high: for example, 15% of the babies being born at the Saweto Baragawanath hospital are born HIV positive.[8]
* Because of the isolation from apartheid many are uneducated about AIDS.[9]

Homosexuality

* Homosexuality is illegal.[9]
* The military feels homosexuality is considered a psychiatric problem, and it also reports cultural disapproval for at least some forms of homosexual behavior.[10]
* Since the change of government, homosexual couples are out in the open more than before.[10]

Prostitution[11]

* Prostitution is illegal.
* There are prostitutes on the streets, but the police don't have the resources to combat it.

Pornography[12]

* Pornography is illegal, but the government doesn't enforce the law.[19]
* In 1994, pictures of women's breast couldn't be published without covering her nipples; however, today explict magazines showing women's breast are made available in supermarkets.[20]

Resources

*Planned Parenthood Association of South Africa, Thrid Floor, Marlborough House, 60 Eloff, Johannesburg, So. Africa, 2001

References

1. D. Lucas, "Fertility and Family Planning in Southern and Central Africa," <u>Studies in Family Planning</u> (May/June 1992), vol. 23(3), p. 31-39.

2. "Apartied Gone, Anything Goes," <u>The New York Times</u> (December 28, 1994), v144, p. A7.

3. O. Dan, "Population Studies in South Africa," <u>Studies in Family Planning</u> (Jan/Feb 1993), vol 24(3), p.

4. C. Ellertson et al, "Expanding Access to Emergency Contraception in Developing Countries," <u>Studies in Family Planning</u> (Sept/Oct. 1995), vol. 26(5), p. 251-263.

5. S. Pachev, "Republic of South Africa," <u>International Handbook on Abortion</u> (New York, 1988), p. 416-424.

6. L. Schmittroth, <u>Statistical Record of Women Worldwide</u>. New York: Gale Research, 1995, p. 614, Table 642.

7. United Nations, <u>Statistical Yearbook</u> (New York, 1995), p. 94.

8. L. Doyle, "Opening of South Africa Brings Rapid Advance of AIDS," <u>The Washington Post</u> (July 23, 1995), v118, p. A16.

9. "AIDS Cases Spread Rapidly Among Black Homosexuals in South Africa," <u>The New York Times</u> (September 27, 1990), v1400, p. A12.

10. S. Harris, "Military Policies Regarding Homosexual Behavior: An International Study," <u>Journal of Homosexuality</u> (1991), v21, p. 67-74.

11. "Prostitution" http://www/paranoia.com/faq/prostitution/south africa.html (retrieved June 17, 1996)

12. K. Wells, "The New South Africa Sheds Calvanist Past and Mutates Daily," <u>The Wall Street Journal</u> (June 9, 1995), p. A1.

SPAIN
POPULATION: 39.5 MILLION

Capital:
Madrid
(population: 2.9 million)

Major Cities & Population:	Madrid 2.9 million; Barcelona .6 million; Valencia 753,000; Serville 659,000; Zaragoza 596,000
Ethnic Groups:	Spanish Castilian 73%; Catalan 16%; Galician 7%; Basque 2%
Languages:	Castilian Spanish, Basque, Catalan, Galician
Major Religions:	Roman Catholic 99%
Annual Income per Person:	$12,460
Urban Population:	64%
Infant Mortality:	7 per 1,000
Life Expectancy:	Females 81 years; Males 75 years
Adult Literacy:	97%
Health Care System:	Private Physicians 1 per 257; health centers

References:
Encyclopedic World Atlas (1994) NY: Oxford University Press.
The World Almanac and Book of Facts 1996 (1995) Mahwah, NJ: World Almanac Books.

Sexual Activity

* Legal age of consent for heterosexual relations is 12.[1]
* Typical age of first intercourse: 16.5 years old.[2]
* According to a recent study, almost 30% of 15-19 year olds have had first sexual interocurse in an "at-risk" situation (either because they were not using any method of contraception or because the methods they were using were inadequate).[2]

Contraception

* Contraceptive use was officially legalized in 1978.[3]
* Most common methods of contraception: Barrier (14%), Pill (12%), IUD (8%); 16% report no method.[3]
* Emergency contraception is available without consulting a doctor or having a prescription.[4]
* Due to the high rate of unprotected sex among adolescents (despite availability of contraceptives), emergency contraception is in high demand. For example, one family planning clinic for youth found that 25% of of clients contact the clinic for this method.[4]

Abortion

* Since 1985, abortion has been legally permitted on limited grounds: when the pregnancy presents a serious risk to the mother, rape (up to 12 weeks), and fetal abnormalities (up to 22 weeks).[5]
* Efforts to liberalize abortion (e.g., allow abortion on request until the 12th week) have been made.[6]
* Most abortions (95%) are carried out in private clinics where women pay for the abortion themselves (35,000-60,000 pesetas or US$350-600).[7]

Sex Education[2]

* The Ministry of Social Affairs subsidised the opening of three Youth Contraception and Sexuality Centres (in Barcelona, Santiago, and Madrid) to educate youth about contraception and sexuality issues.

* Once a taboo subject, sexuality is now present on television, in cinema and in magazines, and it has been included in official education programs.
* In 1990, the Law of General Arrangement of the Education System was passed which included to need to provide sex education as part of health ediucation.

STDs, including AIDS

* AIDS cases: 40,945 cases.[8]
* Spain has the highest number of new AIDS cases of any European country.[9]

Homosexuality

* The age of consent is 12 for lesbians and gays; this is the lowest age of consent in Europe.[10]
* There is a law against gay men and lesbian women showing affection in public.[11]
* Gays are accepted in the military.[12]

Prostitution

* Legal situation is unknown.[13]

Pornography

* No information available.

Resources

*Federacion de Planificacion Familiar de Espana, Almagro 28, 28010 Madrid
*Federacion Espanola de Sociedades de Sexologia, c/Valencians, 6-Principal, 46002, Valencia.
*Societat Catalan de Sexologia, Tren de Baix, 51, 2o, 2o, 08223 Teraessa, Barcelona.
*Sociedad Sexologica de Madrid, c/Barbieri, 33 dcha, 28004, Madrid.

References

1. Alan F. Reekie, "Age of Consent Laws in the Council of Europe States in 1993," <http://ftp.tcp.com/qrd/world/europe/age.of.consent.laws-12.20.94>.

2. E. Nieto & L. DeCiria, "FPA Youth Programme in Spain," Choices, (1996), 25(1), p. 5-7.

3. M. Perez & M. Livi-Bacci, "Fertility in Italy and Spain: The Lowest in the World," Family Planning Perspectives (1992), 24(4), p. 162-171.

4. R. Perez, "Emergency Contraception at a Youth Service Centre," Planned Parenthood in Europe (1995), 24(2), p. 11-12.

5. National Abortion Campaign, Abortion Laws in Europe (London, 1995).
6. I. Fuster, "Spain about to Change Its Abortion Law," Planned Parenthood in Europe (1994), 23(3), p. 27-28.

7. M. Gasco, "Spain Still in Need of a Good Aboriton Law," Planned Parenthood in Europe (1991), 20(2), p. 15-17.

8. HIV.NET "Epidemiology: Transmission Cases" http://www.hiv.net (retrieved June 26, 1996)

9. M. Rebagliatl, "Trends in In cidence and Prevalence of HIV-1 Infection in IV Drug Users in Valencia Spain," Journal of AIDS & Human Retrovirology (1996), 8(3), p. 297.

10. P.Snyder, The European Woman's Almanac (NY: Columbia University Press, 1992), p. 129.

11. A. Duda, "Comparative Survey of the Legal and Societal Situation of Homosexuals in Europe," http://www.casti.com/FQRD/assocs/ilga/euroletter/35-survey.html (retrieved June 26, 1996).

12. "Gay Sailors Blaze Path for Others: Return to Base After Court Order," New York Times (Nov. 3, 1992), p. A12.

13. The World Sex Guide. Last updated 1996/04/30. (C) 1994, 1995, 1996 Atta and M. <an48932@anon.penet.fi> (retrieved June 26, 1996).

SWEDEN
POPULATION: 9 MILLION

Capital:
Stockholm
(population: 1.5 million)

Major cities & Populations:	Stockholm 1.5 million, Goteborg 720,000 Malmo 500,000, Uppsala 162,000
Ethnic Groups:	Swedish 90%; Finnish 2%; Lapps, European immigrants
Languages:	Swedish (official), Finnish
Major Religions:	Evangelical Lutheran 94%; Protestant & Roman Catholic
Annual Income Per Person:	$25,490
Urban Population:	83%
Infant Mortality:	6 per 1,000
Life Expectancy:	Female 81 years; Male 76 years
Adult Literacy:	100%
Health Care System:	Physicians: 1 per 394 persons

References:
Encyclopedic World Atlas (1994) NY: Oxford University Press.
The World Almanac and Book of Facts 1996 (1995) Mahwah, NJ: World Almanac Books

Sexual Activity

* For the past 25 years, Sweden has had very liberal attitudes towards teenage sexuality.[1]
* There are no parental rights when it comes to the sexuality of minor women, except below the age of 15. A young Swedish woman can independently decide whether she wants to have a boyfriend, have sex with him, have contraceptives or even have an abortion.[1]
* In Sweden, youngsters lose thier virginity at age 17.[2]

Contraception

* Contraception was legalized in 1938.[3]
* Contraceptives are easily accessible, affordable and available to anyone, regardless of age or marital status. Such accessibility has proven effective in the prevention of teen pregnancy. For example, only 35 babies were born to mothers under 16 in 1993.[1]
* Permission from parents, other guardian or husband is not needed, and there are no religious prohibitions against contraceptives.[1]
* Youth Clinics in every community offer free, confidential services and counseling in sexual matters to young people.[1]
* Midwives provide about 80% of all contraceptive counseling.[4]
* Anyone who is over 25 and a Swedish citizen or legal resident can be sterilized on request.[3]
* Birth control pills are free for the first 3 months. The cost of a year supply of oral contraception is approximately 320 Swedish crowns(SEK), approximately US $40.[5]
* Since 1990, the RFSU clinic has advocated emergency contraception by offering the service and information to both professionals and the general public. During 1992-1994 there were 346 visitors for post-coital contraception (PCC) at the RFSU clinic.[4]
* Emergency contraception is marketed under various names by Schering AG as a four pill strip with its own package insert.[6]

Abortion

* Available on request up to 12 weeks on consultation with a doctor, between 12 and 18 weeks on consultation with a doctor and a counselor, and after 18 weeks with the approval of the National Board of Health and Welfare.[3]
* Sweden has one of the lowest numbers of abortions in the world.[1]

* Abortion is free. It is paid for by public social security insurance; the estimated price for an abortion is SEK 5,000 (US $625).[7]
* Sweden now has access to RU 486, the so-called "abortion pill" which must be taken within 63 days after conception has occured.[8]

Sex   Education

* Sex education has been a compulsory subject in Swedish schools since 1955. Sex education starts at the age of seven, in the first grade, and then is brought up on a recurring basis for approximately 15 hours per year.[1]
* Swedish children receive their first sex education at home, from their parents.[9]
* Sex education is well integrated in school curricula.[10]

STDs, including AIDS

* Sweden has a very successful STD program which provides free STD diagnosis and treatment, partner notification, sex education in schools, publicity about high gonorrhea rates and condom promotion.[1]
* The incidence of gonorrhea decreased from 487 to 31 cases per 100,000 population between 1970 and 1987; the number of cases of chlamydia almost halved between 1986 and 1991.[11]
* AIDS cases: 1,315.[12]
* Age of consent for homosexual and lesbian relations is 15.[13]

Homosexuality

* The Partnership Act was passed through the Riksdag in 1994. This means that homosexual couples who contract a partnership with each other have broadly the same rights as heterosexual couples who contract a marriage with each other. There are some exceptions, for example, homosexual couples are not allowed to adopt children.[14]
* The Swedish Federation for Gay and Lesbian Rights reports that more and more lebian women are conceiving children through self-insemination with sperm donated from a gay male friend, and with joint custody of the child.[3]
* Sweden has no policy excluding persons who engage in homosexual behavior from military service.[15]

169

Prostitution

* Prostitution is legal for both males and females, although in 1995 a Prostitution Act was proposed and debated to criminalize both the prostitute and the customer.[1]
* Pimping, brothels and live shows are illegal.[16]

Pornography

* The sale of child pornography is illegal as are pornographic shows and exposure of pornographic pictures in shop windows.[1]
* Pornographic material is widely available.[2]

Resources

*RFSU, P.O. Box 12128, Drottningholmsvagen 37, Stockholm 102 24   Tel: (46 8) 692 0700;

References

1. The Danish FPA & Swedish RFSU, <u>The Sexual Rights of Young Women in Denmark and Sweden</u> (Denmark: Clausen Offset, 1995), p. 9-23.

2. G. Kelly, Sexuality Today, (Guilford, CT: Brown & Benchmark, 1995), p. 247 & 446.

3. P. Snyder, <u>European Women's Almanac</u> (New York: Columbia Univ. Press: 1992), p. 330-332.

4. C. Rogala & B. Anzen, "Late Start for Emergency Contraception in Sweden," <u>Planned Parenthood in Europe</u> (1995), 24(2), p. 15-17.

5. E. Persson et al, "Subsidizing Contraeption for Young People in Sweden, <u>Planned Parenthood in Europe</u> (1994), 23(1), p. 2-4.

6. C. Ellertson et al, "Expanding Access to Emergency Contraception in Developing Countries," <u>Studies in Family Planning</u> (1995), 26(5), p. 257.

7. E. Persson et al, "Subsidizing Contraeption for Young People in Sweden, <u>Planned Parenthood in Europe</u> (1994), 23(1), p. 2-4.

8. B. Rolston & A. Eggers, <u>Abortion in the New Europe</u> (Westport, CT: Greenwood, 1994), p. 247.

9. M. Bygdeman & K. Lindahl, <u>Sex Education and Reproductive Health in Sweden in the 21st Century</u> (Swedish Government Offical Report, 1994), p. 49.

10. D. Vilar, "School Sex Education: Still a Priority in Europe," <u>Planned Parenthood in Europe</u> (1994), 23(3), p. 8-12.

11. Population Information Program, <u>Controlling STDs</u>, (June 1993), Series L, # 9, p. 7.

12. http://www.hiv.net (retrieved June 25, 1996).

13. Alan F. Reekie, "Age of Consent Laws in the Council of Europe States in 1993," <http://ftp.tcp.com/qrd/world/europe/age.of.consent.laws-12.20.94>.

14. RFSU, <u>Annual Report</u> (Stockholm, 1994).

15. S. Harris, "Military Policies Regarding Homosexual Behavior: An International Survey," <u>Journal of Homosexuality</u> (1991), 21(4), p. 67-74.

16. <u>The World Sex Guide</u> last update 1996/04/30 (c) 1994, 1995, 1996, Atta & M. <An48932@anon.penet.fi> (retrieved June 25, 1996).

SWITZERLAND
POPULATION: 6.9 MILLION

Capital:
B e r n
(population: 135,000)

Major Cities & Populations: Zurich 340,000; Basel 170,000; Geneva 170,000; Lausanne 123,000

Ethnic Groups: Germanic, French, Italian, Rhaeto-Romansch

Languages: Schweizerdeutch (Swiss German), French, Italian, Romansch

Major Religions: Roman Catholic (48%); Protestant (44%)

Income Per Capita: $36,230

Urban Population: 68%

Infant Mortality: 6 per 1000 births

Life Expectancy: Women 82 years, men 75 years

Adult Literacy: 100%

Health Care System: Excellent, major producer of specialized pharmaceutical products

---

References:
Worldmark Encyclopedia of the Nations: Europe, Vol. 5, Eighth Edition, pp. 429-437, Gale Research Inc, Detroit, 1995.
The World Almanac and Book of Facts 1996 (1995), Mahwah, NJ: World Almanac Books

Sexual   Activity

* Age of consent in Switzerland is 16.[1]
* It is an offense for adult males to seduce adolescents between the ages of 16 and 20, though there have been government recommendations to repeal this section of the penal code.[1]
* Sexual activity between consenting minors whose age difference is less than three years will not be prosecuted.[2]

Contraception

* Pro-choice groups are attempting to introduce RU-486.[3]
* High school students have recently requested condom availability in schools.[3]
* There are numerous family planning centers throughout the country, some for counseling only, but others offering gynecological exams and contraception.[3]
* Adolescents can easily obtain birth control.[3]
* 78% of Pro Familia's patients who had had abortions decided to use the Pill.[4]

Abortion

* Abortion is legal until fetal viability, and if there is risk to the woman's life, physical health, or mental health.[5]
* Must consult with a second, specialized doctor.[5]
* Abortion is generally covered by health insurance, though woman must pay something, depending on the type of insurance.[5]
* There are regional differences in availability of services.[5]
* Current laws were passed in 1942.[3]
* No parental consent for minors.[3]
* No mandatory counseling.[3]
* No waiting period.[3]
* Many cantons are very liberal in their abortion policies, though a few are extremely restrictive, causing women to travel to the more liberal areas of Switzerland.[3]
* For every 6 births there is one legal abortion.[3]
* Requests for pregnancy termination are declining among the general population, as well as among the adolescent population.[4]
* Only about 30% of patients seeking abortion at the family planning section of the Centre medico-social Pro Familia were adolescents. 19% of these women said that they became pregnant despite regular condom use.[4]

173

Sex Education[6]

* A group called Women and AIDS develops all information for females. This group works without any funding from Swiss AIDS.
* The Stop AIDS campaign attempts to reach the whole population by 'sympathetically understanding the everyday situations of people and creating messages everyone can identify with.
* Stop AIDS's nationwide attempts to provide AIDS education include billboards and television ads discussing condom use, as well as a soft-porn video demonstrating the use of condoms.

STDs, including AIDS[7]

* There have been 5,275 documented AIDS cases in Switzerland since 1984, primarily by IV drug users and homosexuals.
* There have been 789 per million people diagnosed with AIDS.

Homosexuality

* Recent referendums in Switzerland were held. One of the results was that the age of consent for homosexuals is no longer different from that of heterosexuals.[1]
* There is no longer any military discrimination against homosexuals, as long as "their behavior does not disturb the discipline of military life."[8]
* In 1995, a petition was brought to the Parliament by the national gay and lesbian organization, Pink Cross, seeking partnership rights for homosexuals.[9]

Prostitution

* For every 1.5 prostitutes, there are 98.5 clients.[6]
* Prostitution is legal, and prostitutes must register with the authorities.[10]
* In certain areas, street prostitution is banned.[10]
* Brothels are legal, but brothel owners may be prosecuted as pimps.[10]
* Massage parlors and studios are common, as well as street prostitution and call girls.[10]
* Advertisements can be found in daily newspapers, such as *Blick* and *TagesAnzeiger*, centered in Zurich.[10]
* Magazines such as *OSA*, *Okay* and *Sex-Anzeiger* also contain information about prostitution.[10]

Pornography[2]

* Pornography is illegal, though soft pornography is tolerated. Hard pornography, dealing with children, animals, excrement or violence is illegal.

Resources

*Association Suisse de Planning Familail et d'Education Sexuelle (ASPFES), Gueta 7, 1073 Savigny, Switzerland.

References

1. Alan F. Reekie, "Age of Consent Laws in the Council of Europe States in 1993," <http://ftp.tcp.com/qrd/world/europe/age.of.consent.laws-12.20.94>.

2. <http://www.nz.qrd.org/world/europe/switzerland/referendum.on.sexual.equality.passes>, retrieved 6/12/96.

3. Bill Rolston and Anna Eggert, <u>Abortion in the New Europe: A Comparative Handbook</u>, Switzerland, p. 262, 263, Greenwood Press, Westport, CT, 1984.

4. Mary Anna Barbey, "Switzerland: Induced Abortion is on the Wane, Even Among Adolescents," <u>Planned Parenthood in Europe</u>, Vol. 22, No. 3, 1993, p. 17.

5. <u>National Abortion Campaign</u>, "Abortion Laws in Europe," (amended Jan 1995), p. 4, London, England.

6. "AIDS and Women: A Swiss Perspective," <u>Feminist Review</u> #41, Summer 1992, p. 58-63.

7 <u>HIV.NET</u>, http://www.hiv.net, 6/19/96

8. Stanley E. Harris, MD, "Military Policies Regarding Homosexual Behavior, An International Survey, <u>Journal of Homosexuality</u>, Vol.21, 1991, Haworth Press, inc. P. 70,71.

9. Frederic Ballenegger, <http://www.qrd.org/qrd/world/europe/switzerland/partnership.news.03.27.96>.

10. <u>The World Sex Guide</u>, "Prostitution in Switzerland," <http://www.paranoia.com/faq/prostitution/Switzerland.html>, 4/30/96.

THAILAND
Population: 60.2 MILLION

Capital:
Bangkok
(population: 5,609,000)

Major Cities & Populations:	Bangkok, 5,609,000; Nakhon Ratchasima 191,000; Chiang Mai 151,000
Ethnic Groups:	Thai 75%; Chinese 14%
Languages	Thai (official), Chinese, Malay
Major Religions:	Buddhist 95%; Muslim 4%
Annual Income per Person:	$1,580
Urban Population:	19%
Infant Mortality:	36 per 1000 live births (1995)
Life Expectancy:	Females 72 years; Males 65 years
Adult Literacy:	91%
Health Care System:	1 doctor for 4,327 people; volunteer health organizations, private market government, hospitals, government health centers, traditional healers.

References:
Encyclopedic World Atlas (1994) NY: Oxford University Press
National Health Systems of the World, Vol. 1, (1991) NY: Oxford University Press
The World Almanac and Book of Facts 1996 (1995) Mahwah, NJ: World Almanac Books

Sexual   Activity

* Premarital sex between men and women who are dating is strictly forbidden.[1]
* Love affairs, premarital pregnancy and abortions are not uncommon, but discovery is the major issue at stake.[2]
* Public discussion of sexual behavior is "taboo".[3]
* Cash payments is often used to compensate the girl's parents when sexual relations outside of marriage occur.[2]
* Pregnancy for an unmarried woman brings shame to both her and her family.[2]
* Women are expected to be chaste until marriage and monogamous afterward.[1]
* "Good" Thai women are expected to minimize their sexual activity.[4]
* Sex for Thai males is a means of releasing a bodily need, and of achieving pleasure.[3]
* Men have more sexual freedom than women, this is not only permitted but expected.[5]
* Marriage is not for love and companionship as much as it is done for economic reasons and to produce children.[3]
* Among Thai men polygamous relationships and frequenting prostitutes is common.[5]

Contraception

The most prevalent method of birth control is female sterilization, followed by the Pill. The least popular method is the condom.[5]
* Oral contraceptives, injectables and IUDs are modern methods that have helped slow the population growth of Thailand.[5]
* Women bear the responsibility of reproductive and productive obligations.[5]
* Between 1989 and 1993 the use of condoms in commercial sex increased from 14 to 94%.[6]

Abortion[5]

* Abortion is technically illegal except in cases of rape or threat to the woman's health.
* Abortion is often the chosen method in cases of premarital pregnancy; either done in an urban clinic or by traditional methods of ingesting "hot" medicine or forceful massage. These methods are extremely painful and detrimental to the woman's health.

Sex Education

* A National AIDS Committee was formed to help wage a nationwide AIDS education campaign with condom use as the centerpiece for the campaign.[1]
* Motivation for Safer Sex for Youth in Rural Communities is set up to motivate youth to practice safer sex by: consistent use of condoms, reducing sexual partners, discouraging visits to brothels and negotiating for safer sex.[7]
* Samutprakarn AIDS Prevention project was developed to offer short-training sessions for industrial workers on HIV/AIDS prevention.[7]
* Health official routinely visit brothels to educate sex workers.[1]
* With strong taboos surrounding the discussion of sex and disease AIDS education has been stifled and many do not know how the disease is spread.[8]

STDs, including AIDS

* In 1984, the first case of AIDS was reported tot he Ministry of Public Health.[9]
* The Thai government was slow in responding to HIV/AIDS since the disease was associated with both Westerners and gays.[5]
* Thai government began an HIV-control program in 1989, they bought and distributed condoms to protect much of the commercial sex in the country, brought sanctions against sex establishments that did not use condoms consistently, and the media bluntly advised men not to have sex with prostitutes without using condoms.[5]
* From 1989-1993 the number of male cases of the five classic STD's declined by 79%.[6]
* Sexually transmitted diseases including HIV/AIDS are a grave threat to all women in Thailand as long as male partners continue to frequent brothels and other sex establishments while maintaining steady relationships.[5]
* Thailand's population is highly mobile in order to maintain economic survival, this has contributed to the rapid spread of the HIV infection.[5]
* Girls aged 10-14 have the highest rates or rural-urban migration, HIV infection rate in child prostitutes is now approaching 50%.[10]
* 40-80% of all female commercial sex workers working in brothels are now HIV seropositive.[11]
* In 1995 Thailand had 800,000 of Asia's 3 million reported HIV cases.[12]

Homosexuality

* Homosexuality is not condemned or treated in any special way in Thailand.[13]
* There are no laws against homosexuality[5] yet there are laws on consent, 15 years for relations between local guys and 18 years for commercial sex, as with foreigners.[15]
* There is approximately 1 million homosexuals in Thailand, one of the highest rates in the world.[3]
* Like other sexual behaviors homosexuality is seldom discussed in public.[3]
* Thais do not set apart those males who choose to have sex with other males, as long as they conform to heterosexual norms long enough to get married and have children. He then may continue to have sex with other males without being considered socially deviant.[3]

Prostitution

* In 1960 the Prohibiting Prostitution Act was passed making prostitution, brothel keeping, and procurement illegal in Thailand.[2]
* In 1966 the Entertainment Places Act offered an alternative to the old style brothels: massage parlours, nightclubs, bars, coffee shops, tea houses and barber shops.[2]
* During the Vietnam War Thailand was the R&R center for the American troops. The sex industry was so well established that after the war ended Thailand had to attract an alternative clientele or disemploy thousands of workers.[16]
* Female sexuality plays a critical role in Thailand's economic development and growth.[5] Prostitution is looked at as a means to support the family and provide for basic material needs.[2]
* The commercial sex industry is ruled by the cold, hard laws of economics, new money and changing tastes are bringing younger and younger girls and boys into the business. There is an estimated 100,000 children under the age of 18 working as prostitutes.[17]
* Thailand is the international symbol of the child prostitution problem, it is a place where children are disposable, dragged out of school as early as 6th grade, their virginity sold by their parents to brothels.[18]
* 75% of all men have had sex with a prostitute.[10]

Pornography

* Legal age for viewing pornography is 18 years.[19]
* Pornography is largely thought of as published materials: books, magazines, and photographs, this is not the case in Thailand where live sex shows, dances, strip and peep shows go on daily.[2]
* Shows include single, duo and trio acts. Single acts focus on the vagina, which include act that focus on pelvic-floor control; and include smoking cigarettes, blowing out candles, and insertion and release of ping-pong balls. Duo and trio acts follow along the same acts as single but with the additional people. There are bars that sexual intercourse, heterosexual or lesbian is performed.[2]

Resources

*Planned Parenthood Association of Thailand, 8 Soi Dai Dee, Vibhavadi-Rangsit Super Hwy., Lard-Yao, Bangkhen, Bangkok 9, Thailand Tel: 2 5790084 or 2 5790086.
*Population and Community Development Association, 8 Sukhumvit Rd., SOI-12, Bangkok 10110, Thailand Tel: 2 2560080 or 2 2558804.
*United Nations Family Planning Association (UNFRA)-East and Southeast Asia Region Office, Population Education Clearinghouse, United Nations Building, Rajdammnern Avenue, Bangkok 10200 Thailand

References

1. R. Moreau, "Sex and Death in Thailand," Newsweek, (July 20, 1992), pp. 50-51.
2. L. Manderson, "Public Sex Performances in Patpong and Explorations of the Edges of Imagination," The Journal of Sex Research, (November, 1992), Vol. 29, pp. 451-475.
3. P. Jackson, "Male Homosexuality in Thailand: An Interpretation of Contemporary Thai Sources," (Elmhurst, NY: Global Academic Publishers, 1989), pp. Index - 284.
4. Editorial, "Where is the solution?" Bangkok Post, (July 5, 1994), p. 4.
5. H. Pyne, "Reproductive Experiences and Needs of Thai Women: Where Has Development Taken Us?" Power and Decision: The Social Control of Reproduction, (Boston, MA: Harvard University Press, 1994), pp. 19-41.
6. R. Hanenberg, W. Rojanapithayakorn, P. Kunasol, and D. Sokal, "Impact of Thailand's HIV-control programme as indicated by the decline of sexually transmitted diseases," Lancet, (July 23, 1994), Vol. 344, pp. 243-45.
7. http://www.care.org/world/profiles/thailand.html, Care - Thailand, (06/14/96), pp. 1-3.
8. "AIDS infection soars in Asia," Contemporary Sexuality, (Feb. 1993), V. 27 n2, p. 4.
9. http://www.nectec.or.th/users/craig/history.html, "Historical Overview of HIV/AIDS in Thailand", (06/16/96), pp. 1-4.
10. A. Sachs, "The Last Commodity: Child Prostitution in the Developing World," World Watch, (Jul-Aug, 1994), Vol. 7, n4, pp. 24-30.
11. D.D. Celentano, et. al., "Dynamics of Risk Behavior for HIV infection among Young Thai Men," Journal of Acquired Immune Deficiency Syndromes and Human Retrovirology, (December 1, 1995) Vol. 10, n4, pp. 477-483.
12. "AIDS Counting the Cost," The Economist, (September 23, 1995), pp. 26-27.
13. W. Dynes, Encyclopedia of Homosexuality, (NY: Garland Publishing Inc., 1990), Vol. 2, l. 1329-1330.
14. http://www.qrd.org/world/asia/thailand/the/gay.heaven, "Thailand the Gay Heaven" (06/18/96), pp. 1-3.
15. http://www.c2.net/~prd/world/Asia/aocLaws.txt, (06/27/96), p. 1.
16. J. Seabrook, "Sex for Sale, Cheap Thrills," New Statesman & Society, (May 31, 1991), pp. 12-13.
17. A. Shetry, M. Lee, and M. Vatiklotis, "Sex Trade: For Lust of Money", Far Eastern Economic Review, (December 14, 1995), pp. 22-23.
18. B. Hebert, "Kids for Sale," The New York Times, (Jan. 22, 1996), Vol. 145, p. A15.
19. http://www.pinkboard.com.au:80/r.html, "Legal age for viewing pornography," (06/19/96).

TURKEY
POPULATION: 62.5 MILLION

Capital:
A n k a r a
(population: 3.8 million)

Major Cities & Populations: Istanbul 11.4 million; Ankara 3.8 million; Izmir 2.9 million; Adana 776,000

Ethnic Groups: Turk 80%, Kurd 20%

Languages: Turkish (official), Kurdish

Major Religions: Muslim 99.8%

Annual Income per Person: $1,820

Urban Population: 64%

Infant Mortality: 46 per 1,000 live births

Life Expectancy: Females 74 years; Males 69 years

Adult Literacy: 79%

Health Care System: 1 doctor per 1,974 people; National Health Care sytem, government hospitals, health centers, health houses and the private health care market.

References:
Encylopedic World Atlas (1994) NY: Oxford University Press
Information Please Almanac, Atlas and Yearbook 1996 49th Ed. (1996) Boston, MA: Hougton Mifflin Co.
The World Almanac and Book of Facts 1996 (1995) Mahwah, NJ: World Almanac Books

Sexual Activity

* Illegal virginity tests are commonly conducted on unmarried women who are in police detention, or women who are applying for government jobs. These tests were also administered to "suspicious" female students in schools. The tests are no longer allowed to be given in schools as of February, 1995.[1]
* An intact hymen is "the most valuable piece of a girl's trousseau" for Turkish men.[2]
* Women who have broke the cardinal rule of purity are sent back to their parents' home where "she will carry her shame to her grave", and receive rough treatment by her unforgiving family.[2]
* Men are usually unconcerned and shrug off any responsibility for their part in the lose of virginity to an unmarried woman.[2]
* At least 12 percent of all murders committed in Turkish cities are caused by sexual jealousy.[2]
* Age of consent for heterosexual relations is 18.[3]

Contraception

* Turkish women bear of brunt of responsibility for birth control. Condoms are not popular among Turkish men and campaigns to encourage vasectomies have proved a failure.[4]
* Withdrawal is the most common form of birth control practiced among couples in Turkey.[5] Fear of health related problems, side effects, and husbands opposition are reasons most commonly given for not using modern methods.[6]
* Many women believe that withdrawal is at least as effective as modern methods of contraception and with fear of health related problems and out of date information on oral contraceptives the failure rate at times has for this method has been higher for then for the traditional method of withdrawal.[6]
* Only one-third of the women use modern contraceptives.[7]

Abortion

* Abortion has become more frequent since 1983, when abortion became available upon request.[8]
* Abortions on request up to10 weeks, over 10 weeks in cases of: risk to woman's life or risk to fetal health or handicap. A report from two specialist in cases of risk to woman or fetus health.[9]

* Married women need consent from their husbands and minors need consent from parents, guardian or magistrate's court.[9]
* Women, age 35 to 39, are most likely to terminate a pregnancy.[10]
* 1 in every 4 pregnancies is terminated by induced abortion.[11]
* 500,000 abortions are performed annually.[12]
* The cost of a State abortion is $10.00, the cost of a private abortion is $100.[12]

Sex Education

* Sex Education Task Force established to convince Ministry of National Education that sex education needs to become a priority. Turkey has a large population of young people.[10]
* Authorities in Turkey tend to ignore the fact that children should receive sexual education. Scientific works and the reading of such works are limited in distribution.[11]
* In 1990, FPAT was the first organization in Turkey to establish the project, the Youth to Youth Family Health Project. It aimed to reach 10,000 University students through the community based peer education, with information on family planning, family health, STDs and AIDS.[10]

STDs, including AIDS

* High prevalence of syphilis among both Turkish and immigrant female prostitutes in Istanbul, and high rates of syphilis among male prostitutes.[13]
* Patterns of health care seeking behaviors and provision of STD clinical services indicate that other STDs may play a very important role in the spread of HIV infection in Turkey.[13]
* 122 AIDS cases in Turkey.[14]

Homosexuality

* Age of consent for homosexual and lesbian relations is 18.[3]
* Sisters of Venus, the first and only Turkish lesbian group was established in July 1994.[15]
* Sisters of Venus is helping to report on women's legal situation in Turkey, including a comprehensive report on lesbians' right. They are also working on educational material on AIDS for Turkish women.[15]

* Same-sex love can be found in Turkish history as far back as 1207, when the great Sufi poet Jelal al-Din Rumi, held a passion for youth.[16]
* There are no Turkish laws that make is a crime to be a homosexual or to lead a homosexual life, still gay people conceal their homosexuality.[11]
* The city of Istanbul is thought to have nearly half a million homosexuals living there.[16]

Prostitution

* Prostitution is illegal but tolerated in Turkey.[17]
* Women from Romania and Russia are coming to Turkey to trade sexual favors to earn money for a legitimate business back home, this is called the `Natasha Syndrome'.[17]
* There are both male[16] and female brothels.[18]
* Some brothels are legal, women who work there must have legal licenses and are supervised by police doctors and given clean bills of health.[18]

Pornography

* As of February 6, 1996 it is no longer a punishable offense to bring pornographic magazines to schools.[15]
* Modest additions of Penthouse and similar magazines are now sold at newsstands, bolder ones in white cellophane covers.[17]
* Private Turkish and foreign satellite television stations have begun to beam in naughtier fare than the state-run stations.[17]

Resources

*Family Planning Association of Turkey, Atac Sokak 73/3, 06420 Ankara, Turkey.
*Turkish Family Health & Planning Foundation, Sitesi A Blok D.3-4, 80660 Entiler, Istanbul, Turkey.

References

1. AASECT, "Turkey to revise school virginity tests," <u>Contemporary Sexuality</u>, March (1995) Vol. 29, n3, p. 9.
2. M. Abboud, "Turkey: What Price Virginity?" <u>Connexions</u>, Winter (1992), n38, p. 12.
3. Alan F. Reekie, "Age of Consent Laws in the Council of Europe States in 1993," <http://ftp.tcp.com/qrd/world/europe/age.of.consent.laws-12.20.94>.
4. P. Kandela, "Sexuality goes public in Turkey," <u>The Lancet</u>, July (1990, Vol. 342, p. 42.
5. Bureau of the Census, <u>Population Trends Turkey</u>, (Washington, DC., 1993), pp. 1-4.
6. H. Goldberg and A. Toros, "The Use of Traditional Methods of Contraception among Turkish Couples," <u>Studies in Family Planning</u>, March/April (1994), Vol. 25, n2, pp. 122-128.
7. http://www.macroint.com/dhs/press/tr-rel.html, "Turkey Women Want 2-child Families," (Aug- Oct. 93), 06/26/96.
8. National Abortion Campaign, <u>Abortion laws in Europe (amended Jan. 1995)</u>, (London, England, 1995), pp. 1-4.
9. Bureau of the Census, <u>Population Trends Turkey</u>, (Washington, DC., 1993), pp. 1-4.
10. London International Planned Parenthood 1996, "Sex education in Turkey," <u>Choices</u>, (1996), Vol. 25, n1, p. 39.
11. A. Yuzgan, "Homosexuality and Police Terror in Turkey," <u>Journal of Homosexuality</u>, (Jan.-Feb. 1993), Vol. 24, n3-4, pp. 159-169.
12. L. Schmittroth, <u>Statistical Record of Women Worldwide</u>. New York: Gale Research, 1995, p. 614, Table 642.
13. S.O. Aral and L. Fransen, "STD/HIV Prevention in Turkey: Planning a Sequence of Interventions," <u>AIDS Education and Prevention</u>, (December 1995), Vol. 7 n6, pp. 544-553.
14. United Nations, <u>Statistical Yearbook</u>, (NY: U.N. Publication, 1995), p. 96.
15. "Turkey: feminists, lesbians organize," <u>off our backs</u>, (February 1996), p. 7.
16. W. Dynes, <u>Encyclopedia of Homosexuality</u>, (NY: Garland Publishing Inc., 1990), Vol. 2, l. 1329-1330.
17. A. Cowell, "'Natasha Syndrome' Brings On a Fever in Turkey," <u>NY Times</u>, (April 17, 1993), p. 28L.
18. S. Montefiore, "Call Me Madame," <u>The New Republic</u>, (Aug. 23, 1993), Vol. 209, p. 11.

UNITED KINGDOM
of Great Britian & N. Ireland
POPULATION: 60 MILLION

Capital:
London
(population: 7 million)

Major Cities & Populations	In England (50 M): London 7 million In Scotland (5 M): Edinburgh 0.5 million In Wales (3 M): Cardiff: 0.3 million In N. Ireland (1.5 M): Belfast: 0.3 million
Ethnic Groups:	White 94%; Asian Indian 1%; West Indian 1%; Pakistani 1%
Languages:	English (official), Welsh, Scots-Gaelic
Major Religions:	Anglican 57%; Roman Catholic 13%; Presbyterian 7%; Methodist 4%; Baptist 1%; Muslim 1%; Jewish, Hindu, Sikh
Annual Income per Person:	$16,750
Urban Population:	93%
Infant Mortality:	8 per 1,000 births
Life Expectancy:	Female 79 years; male 73 years
Adult Literacy:	100%
Health Care System:	National health care system

References:
Encyclopedic World Atlas (1994) NY: Oxford University Press.
The World Almanac and Book of Facts 1996 (1995) Mahwah, NJ: World Almanac Books

Sexual Activity

* Typical age of first intercourse: 17 years old.[1]
* A comparison of Western and Northern Europe and the US showed that the UK had the highest teen pregnancy rate, exceeded only by the US.[2]
* In response to the high rate of pregnancies to under 16s, a target has been set to cut the rate in half (from 9.5 per 1,000 to 4.8 per 1,000) by the year 2000.[3]

Contraception

* Increasing numbers of teens are using contraception; fewer than a quarter of women and fewer than half of men reported using no contraception at first intercourse. However, where intercourse occurs before age 16, less than 50% report using contraception.[1]
* Since April 1974, all contraceptive advice provided by the NHS and all prescribed supplies were made available free of charge irrespective of age or marital status.[4]
* Condoms and oral contraceptives are the most popular methods with young people, reported to be used by 60% and 54% respectively.[1]
* Confidentiality: Health professionals can provide contraceptive advice and treatment to those under 16 without parental consent in certain circumstances.[5]
* Mirena, an IUD used widely in Scandinavian countries, was approved for use in the UK in 1995.[6]
* Emergency contraception has been available since 1983; however, a major public education campaign was launched in 1995.[7]

Abortion

* Legal up to 24 weeks, with permission of 2 physicians (however, it is still illegal in Northern Ireland).[8]
* Cost: Despite a national health service, more than 50% of women have to find and pay for their abortions in private clinics.[9]
* Girls under 16 may give written permission to an abortion without parental knowledge, if the doctor feels it is in her best interest.[10]
* RU-486 has been available since 1991.[11]

Sex Education

* In England and Wales, sex education is now required in secondary schools; This change was brought about by Section 241 of the Education Act 1993, which also removed teaching about HIV and other STDs from the National Curriculum and grants parents the right to withdraw their children from any sex education provided other than that covered by the National Curriculum.[12]
* In Scotland, jurisdiction over the provision of sex education lies with the local education authority.[13]
* In Northern Ireland, sex education is not mandated, although is is encouraged in the teaching of health education.[14]
* The Government health strategy, <u>The Health of the Nation</u>, set a number of sexual health targets relating to teen pregnancy and STDs; sex education was idenitfied as one of the central means by which these targets can be achieved.[3]
* Teens report that although they believe their parents should be their main source of information, in practise they are more likely to turn to their friends for sexual information.[15]

STDs, including AIDS

* GUM (Genito-Urinary Medicine) clinics are part of the National Health Service, offering free and confidential medical services. The greatest increase in attendance rates at GUM clincs for women were for herpes, warts, and chlamydia, while there was a decline in gonorrhea and syphilis for men.[16]
* Number of reported AIDS cases: 8,515.[17]
* Of all the HIV infections in the UK, 19% are among people aged 15-24.[18]

Homosexuality

* Consensual sex between men and heterosexual anal intercourse are now legal in the UK providing that the people involved are 18 or over. Homosexual relations were, until the enactment of the Sexual Offenses Act of 1967, entirely illegal (punishment for anal sex was life imprisonment).[19]
* The age of homosexual consent is 18, while the age of heterosexual consent is 16. Recent attempts to change the age of consent from 18 to 16 have been denied.[20]
* An attempt to abolish the government's ban on gays in the military was defeated in 1995.[21]

Prostitution

* Prostitution is technically legal, but several surrounding activities are outlawed which make it hard to work legally. For example, it is illegal to solicit or advertise, run a brothel, or curb-crawl.[22]
* The English Collective of Prostitutes is working to decriminalize prostitution.[23]

Pornography

* The major means of regulation of pornography have been through the *Customs Consolidation Act 1876* (which controls imports), the *Obscene Publications Act 1956* (publishing an obscene article for gain), and the *Indecent Displays Act 1981* (which makes it an offense to display in public material which is indecent or may cause offense or embarrassment to the public).[24]
* The Williams Committee of Great Britian was established in 1977 to review pornography; their conclusion that the effect of pornography was a nuisance rather than harm provided the basis for its recommendation that the principal method of controlling pornography should be to restrict its availability, primarily so that children and young adults and those who had no interest in the material would be less likely to come in contact with it.[25]
* Specific legislation addressing the use if childen in pornography is provided by the Protection of Children Act 1978 (which makes it an offence to publish, distribute or take an indecent photo of a child) and the Criminal Justice Act 1988 (ehich makes it an offence to possess an indecent photo of a child).[24]

Resources

*Family Planning Association of the UK, 2/12 Pentonvlle Road, London N1 9FP ENGLAND.
*Sex Education Forum, National Children's Bureau, 8 Wakely Street, London EC1V 7QU ENGLAND.

References

1. A.M. Johnson, <u>Sexual Attitudes and Lifestyles</u> (Blackwell Scientific, 1994).
2. OPCS, <u>Population Trends</u> (HMSO, 1993), no. 74.
3. Department of Health, <u>The Health of the Nation</u> (HMSO, 1991).
4. K. Wellings, "Trends in Contraceptive Use Since 1970," <u>British Journal of Family Planning</u> (1986), vo. 12, no. 2, p. 15-22.
5. Department of Health and Social Security, <u>Contraceptive Advice and Treatment of Young People Under 16</u>. Health Circular HC (86)1, 1986.
6. Population Information Program, "IUDs - An Update," <u>Population Reports</u> (December 1995), Series B, no. 6, p. 19.
7. K. Pappenheim, "Emergency Contraception Provision in the UK," <u>Planned Parenthood in Europe</u>, vol. 24, no. 2. August 1995, p. 20-22.
8. National Abortion Campaign, <u>Abortion Laws in Europe</u>, (London: NAC, 1995)
9. M. Berer, "Abortion in Europe From a Woman's Perspective," <u>Progress Postponed: Abortion in Europe</u> (London: IPPF, 1993), p. 31-46.
10. Department of Health and Social Security, <u>Family Planning Sevices for Young People</u>, Health Circular HC (86)1, March 1986.
11. W. Smith, "Great Britian Second Country to Allow Use of RU-486," <u>Planned Parenthood in Europe</u> (1991), vol. 20, no. 2, p. 20.
12. Department of Education, <u>Education Act 1993: Sex Education in Schools</u> (1994), Circular 5/94.
13. "Sex Edcuation: A Fact of Life," <u>Children in Scotland Newsletter</u> (1994), 6, p. 1-2.
14. Department of Education of Northern Ireland, <u>Sex Education</u> (1987) Circular 45.
15. K. Rudat, H. Ryan & M. Speed, <u>Today's Young Adults 16 to 19 Year Olds Look at Diet, Alcohol, Drugs & Sexual Behavior</u> (HEA, 1992).
16. Family Planning of the UK, <u>Fact Sheet: STDs: Statistical Trends & Factors Relating to Contraception</u> (London: FPA of UK, 1995).
17. United Nations, <u>Statistical Yearbook</u> (New York, 1995) p. 97.
18. PHLS AIDS Centee and CDEH (s) U, <u>AIDS/HIV Quarterly Surveillance Tables</u> (1994), no 22: Data to end of Dec 1993.
19. Family Planning of the UK, <u>Fact Sheet: Some Laws on Sex</u> (London: FPA of UK, 1995).
20. Department of Health, <u>Criminal Justice & Public Order Act</u> (HMSO, 1994).
21. "British to Keep It's Ban on Homosexuals," <u>The New York Times</u> (1996) v. 145. March 4, p. A6, col. 1.
22. <u>The World Sex Guide</u>. Last update 1996/04/30. (c) 1194, 1995, 1996. Atta and M. <an48932@anon.penet.fi> (retreived June 17, 1996). Web sit: http://www.paranoia.com/faq/prostitution/united kingdom.html
23. A. Holder, "Harsh red lights and boys in blue," <u>The Guardian</u>, (May 12, 1992) p. 36.
24. S. Easton, <u>The Problem of Pornography</u> (London: Routledge, 1994). p. 122-144.
25. E. Einsiedal, "The British, Canadian, and US Pornography Commissions and Their Use of Social Science Research," <u>Journal of Commnication</u> (1988), 38(2), p. 108-111.

UNITED STATES
POPULATION: 250 MILLION

Capital:
Washington, DC
(population: 4 million)

Major Cities & Populations: New York 7 million; Los Angeles 3.5 million; Chicago 2.5 million; Houston 1.5 million; Philadelphia 1.5 million

Ethnic Groups: White 85%; Black 12%, other 3%

Languages: English (official), Spanish and over 30 others

Major Religions: Protestant 55%; Catholic 30%; Jewish 3%; Eastern Orthodox 2%; Muslim 2%

Annual Income per Person: $22,560

Urban Population: 74%

Infant Mortality: 8 per 1,000 births

Life Expectancy: Female 80 years; male 73 years

Adult Literacy: 96%

Health Care System: Private physicians, publicly funded clinics/health centers

---

References:
Encyclopedic World Atlas (1994) NY: Oxford University Press.
The World Almanac and Book of Facts 1996 (1995) Mahwah, NJ: World Almanac Books

Sexual Activity

* Typical age of first intercourse: 16-17 years old.[1]
* 75% of high school seniors report having had sexual intercourse.[2]
* Two-thirds of births to teens are fathered by men 4-6 years older, rather than by their peers.[3]

Contraception

* Since 1968, the government has provided family planning funding (Title X); the 2,500 federally funded family planning agencies operate 5,200 clinic sites, one of the most common providers is Planned Parenthood.[4]
* Parental notification is not required for teens to get birth control.[5]
* Most teens do not use contraception the first few times they have sex.[6]
* Most teens wait an average of one year from first intercourse and their first visit to a family planning clinic.[7]
* Most popular methods: Sterilization 30%; Pill 17%; Condom 10%.[8]
* Emergency Contraception (also called "morning after," "aftersex" or "postcoital" birth control): Available for emergency situations only, although there appears to be more interest in making it more widely available.[9]

Abortion

* Almost 90% of abortions are performed in the first trimester (first 12 weeks) of pregnancy.[8]
* Legislation: Abortion was made legal in a few states in 1970 and throughout the country in 1973 by the Supreme Court. The *Roe v Wade* decision prohibits states from restricting abortion in the first trimester (available at her request) and allows states to regulate abortion to assure its safety in the second trimester and prohibit it, except to save the pregnant women's life or health in the third trimester.[10]
* In subsequent rulings, the Court has upheld the right to abortion, while giving states the right to legislate various kinds of restrictions. For example, state laws have been enacted that require notification of husbands or, in the case of minors, a parent; require a waiting period of up to 24 hours; and/or prohibit the use of pubic facilities for abortions.[11]
* Cost: $260-290 (for first term abortions).[12]
* RU-486 (non-surgical "abortion pill"): Approved for testing/research purposes only. Not available for use by public.[12]

Sex Education

* 47 states either require (23) or encourage (27) teaching about human sexuality and 48 states either require (33) or encourage (15) teaching about HIV/AIDS. However, in many states these mandates or policies preclude teaching about such subjects as intercourse, abortion, masturbation, homosexuality, condoms and safer sex.[13]
* Less than 10% of communities have implemented comprehensive sexuality education.[14]
* The vast majority of Americans support sexuality education. In every opinion poll, more than 8 in 10 parents want sexuality education taught in high schools. Support for HIV/AIDS education is even higher.[13]
* An evaluation of 23 programs found sexuality education programs do not hasten the onset of intercourse, not do they increase the frequency of intercourse or the number of sexual partners; skill-based programs can significantly delay the onset of sexual intercourse and increase contraceptive and condom use among sexually experienced youth.[15]

STDs, including AIDS

* New cases of STDs, which affect 12 million people each year, include:[2]

HIV	40,000
Syphilis	120,000
Hepatitis B	200,000
Genital Herpes	500,000
HPV	1 million
Gonorrhea	1.1 million
Trichomoniasis	3 million
Chlamydia	4 million

* One new HIV infection occurs each 54 seconds; 1 death from AIDS occurs each 9 minutes; 267 new AIDS cases are reported each day.[2]
* In 1995 the total number of AIDS cases passed 500,000. AIDS has been the sixth leading cause of death among 15-24 year olds since 1991.[16]

Homosexuality

* Legislation: In half of all states, nearly all forms of homosexual intimacy involving prevention are still criminal, though prosecutions are rare. *Bowers v Hardwick* (1986) Supreme Court upheld the constitutionality of the Georgia sodomy law, ruling that there was no right to privacy in regard to homosexual behavior.[17]
* Six states in the U.S. have legislation protecting lesbian and gay people against discrimination based on sexual orientation (the first state to pass this legislation was Wisconsin).[18]
* The U.S. military continues to judge homosexuality as incompatible with military service. The *Don't Ask, Don't Tell* policy that was briefly instituted was declared uncoonstitutional by a federal judge 1995.[19]
* The legal status of gay marriage is currently in litigation.[20]

Prostitution

* Prostitution is illegal except in certain counties of Nevada. Visiting a prostitute is also illegal.[19]
* Several organizations are working for the decriminilization of prostitution, including COYOTE, the U.S. Prostitutes Collective, the National Task Force on Prostitution, and the john's JACQUAR.[21]

Pornography

* Pornography, sexually explicit material meant to be sexually arousing, has been subject to many laws throughout recent history. Since 1973, individual states have been allowed to develop their own legislation.[19]
* Pornography is an 8 billion dollar a year business. Half of all adult videos in the U.S. are bought or rented by women alone or women in couples.[22]
* In 1995 the U.S. Senate Commerce Committee proposed banning pornography in cyberspace, and considered the Communications Decency Act, which would make the transmission of "obscene, lewd, lascivious, filthy or indecent" images, e-mail, text files, or other on-line communications punishable by up to $100,000 in fines and 2 years in prison.[23]
* Child pornography is against the law. In 1977, the U.S. passed the Protection of Children Against Sexual Exploitation Act. Since then, those involved in child pornography have been vigorously prosecuted. In 1990, the Supreme Court affirmed the right to prosecute individuals for possession of child pornography (*Osborne v. Ohio*, No. 88-5986).[12]

Resources

*Am. Assoc. of Sex Educators, Counselors & Therapists, P.O. Box 208, Mt. Vernon, IA 52314. Tel: 319/895-8407; Fax: 319/895-6203.

*Planned Parenthood Federation of America, 810 Seventh Avenue, New York, NY 10016.

*Sex Information and Education Council of the United States (SIECUS), 130 West 42nd Street, Suite 2500, New York, NY 10036. Tel: 212/819-9770.

*Society for the Scientific Study of Sexuality (SSSS), P.O. Box 208, Mt. Vernon, IA 52314. Tel: 319/895-8407; Fax: 319/895-6203.

References

1. J. Reinisch, The Kinsey Institute New Report on Sex (New York: St. Martin's).

2. C.A. Dorgan, Statistical Record of Health & Medicine (NY: Gale Research, 1995) Table 48, 315, 316.

3. Contemporary Sexuality (published by AASECT), June 1996, vol. 30, no. 6 p. 6.

4. A. Torres & J. Forrest, "Family Planning Clinic Services in the United States," Family Planning Perspectives, 17 (1985): 30.

5. R. Francoeur, Becoming a Sexual Person (New York: Macmillan Pub) p. 125.

6. R. Crooks & K. Baur, Our Sexuality (Redwood City, CA: Benjamin/Cummings) p. 469.

7. L.S. Zabin & S.D. Clark, "Institutional Factors Affecting Teenagers' Choice and Reasons for Delay In Attending a Family Planning Clinic," Family Planning Perspectives, Jan/Feb (1983).

8. U.S. Census, Statistical Abstract of the U.S, (Washington, DC., 1995) Table 107 & 112.

9. Family Health Council, Public Policy Statement: Post Coital Contraception. (New York, 1996).

10. R.P. Petchesky, Abortion and Women's Choice (Boston: Northeastern University Press, 1985).

11. F.A. Althaus & S.K. Henshaw, "The Effects of Mandatory Delay Laws on Abortion Patients and Providers," Family Planning Perspectives, 25 (1994): 228-233.

12. B. Strong, C. DeVault & B.W. Sayad Core Concepts in Human Sexuality (Mountain View, CA: Mayfield Pub, 1995) . p. 315 & 512.

13. SIECUS "Fact Sheet: Comprehensive Sexuality Education," SIECUS Report, Aug/Sept (1992).

14. National Guidelines Task Force, Guidelines for Comprehensive Sexuality Education (NY: SIECUS, 1991).

15. D. Kirby et al, "School-based Programs to Reduce Sexual Risk Behaviors: A Review of Effectiveness," Public Health Reports, 109 (1994): 339-60.

16. Centers for Disease Control, HIV/AIDS Surveillance Report #7 (U.S. Department of Health and Human Services, Atlanta, GA, 1995).

17. W. Dyne (editor), Encyclopedia of Homosexuality,(NY: Guilford, 1990)

18. SIECUS, "Fact Sheet: Sexual Orientation and Identity," SIECUS Report, Feb/March (1993).

19. G. Kelly, Sexuality Today (Guilford, CT: Brown & Benchmark, 1995) p. 393, 447, 450.

20. K. Hetter,"Gay Issues Bust Out All Over," US News & World Report (Oct. 2, 1995) p. 7.

21. The World Sex Guide. Last update 1996/04/30. (c) 1194, 1995, 1996. Atta and M. <an48932@anon.penet.fi>

22. P. O'Brien, Feminism & Free Spreech: Pornography (NY: Feminists for Free Expression, 1995).

23. S. Levy. "Indecent Proposal: Censor the Net." Newsweek, April 3 (1995) 53.

ZIMBABWE
POPULATION: 11,139,961

Capital:
Harare
(population: 681,000)

Major Cities & Population: Bulawayo 500,000; Chitungwiza, 202,000

Ethnic Groups: African 98% (Shona 71%, Ndebele 16%, other 11%); white 1%; mixed & Asian 1%

Languages: English (official); Shona, Sindebele

Major Religions: Syncretic (part Christian, part indigenous beliefs) 50%; Christian 25%; indigenous beliefs 24%; Muslim 1%

Annual Income Per Person: $1,580

Urban Population: 30%

Infant Mortality: 73 per 1,000

Life Expectancy: Females 43 years, Males 40 yrs

Adult Literacy: 78%

Health Care: 129 doctors, 18 dentists, 40 pharmacists and 592 nurses per 1 million people; 3 hospital beds per 1,000 people. 71% of population has access to health services.

References:
Encyclopedic World Atlas (1994) NY: Oxford University Press.
The World Almanac and Book of Facts 1996 (1995) Mahwah, NJ: World Almanac Books

Sexual   Activity

* All oral and anal sex is prohibited.[1]
* "Multi-partnering" has become a feature of life for all men.[2]

Contraception

* The most commonly used forms of birth control are the pill, injection, condoms and IUD.[3]
* Zimbabwe has one of the highest rates of modern contraception prevalence in Africa; 38%.[4]
* Although condom vending machines are accessible in clubs and bars, there are widespead taboos around the subject of sexuality, making it difficult for individuals to purchase the condoms.[5]
* Condom availability is very inadequate and expensive; the equivalent of five condoms per adult per year are imported.[2]
* Contraceptives are not readily available to women under the age of 18.[6]

Abortion

* Abortion is legal when the woman has been raped or a victim of incest. It is also legal when the fetus has genetic defects.[1]
* It is also legal to save the women's life or preserve physical health.[6]

Sex   Education

* The Zimbabwe National Family Planning Council has been offering programs geared at educating parents of teens on human sexuality.[7]
* Flash cards are used as educational tools to facilitate storytelling about HIV and AIDS.[1]
* Education is becoming more centered around married couples as they are at highest risk of HIV infection.[8]

STD's including AIDS

* As of 9/19/95, there were 41,298 case of AIDS were diagnosed.[9]
* In July 1992, it was estimated that 800,000 people were infected with HIV.[9]
* 30% of pregnant girls ages 15-19 are HIV+.[7]

* Married women account for about 50% of people with AIDS.[10]
* 15% of men and 19% of women have syphilis.[10]
* 18% of men and 10% of women have gonorrhea.[11]

Homosexuality[11]

* President of Zimbabwe, Robert Mugabe, has been known to make anti-homosexual remarks.
* He claims homosexuals have no rights.
* Gays and Lesbians of Zimbabwe is a nationally recognized organization.

Prostitution

* Prostitution is illegal.[10]

Pornography

* No information is available.

Resources

*Zimbabwe National Family Planning Council, P.O. Box 220, Southerton, Harare, Zimbabwe. Tel: 263/667656.

References

1. Sexuality and Gender in Society. (1996). Harper Collins College Pub. pg. 452, 527, 620 - 621.

2. M. Basset, "Zimbabwe: the social roots of AIDS," UNESCO Courier, June (1995).

3. B. Mensch; A. Fisher; I. Askew; A. Ajayi, "Using statistical analysis data to assess the functioning of family planning clinics in Nigeria, Tanzania, and Zimbabwe," Studies in Family Planning. Jan./Feb. (1994).

4. P. Piotrow, et. al. "Changing men's attitudes and behavior: the Zimbabwe male motivational study," Studies in Family Planning, Nov/Dec. (1992).

5. C. Henderson, "Condom vending machine joins fight against AIDS," AIDS Weekly, Sept. (1992).

6. United Nations, Abortion Policies: A Global Review Vol. III, 1995, p. 189-191.

7. Population Reports, Vol. 23, N. 3, Oct. (1995), pg. 12 & 30.

8. D. Munodawafa; C.K. Gwede, "AIDS and HIV surveillance in Zimbabwe: implications for health education." AIDS Weekly, Jan. (1993).

9. The World Health Organization: The Current Global Situation of the HIV/AIDS Pandemic, Dec. (1995).

10. S. Tswana, "Hospital-based study of sexually transmitted diseases at Murewa rural District Hospital, Zimbabwe 1991-1992, Sexually Transmitted Diseases, Jan.-Feb. (1995).

11. M. Gevisser, "Mugabe's mantra," The Nation, Sept. (1995).

AAO-4739

AAO-4739